OFF MARKET

The Absurdity of Real Estate

by

Yvonne M

Contents

*Dedicated to my loving parents who
always believed in me.
Thank you for being you.*

INTRODUCTION

In the cutthroat world of real estate, where laughter and chaos collide, comes a dark comedy that unveils the absurdity and eccentricities lurking behind every property deal. Step into the shoes of a seasoned real estate broker navigating the treacherous landscape of buying, selling, and leasing homes, where transactions take unexpected turns, and people are as unpredictable as the housing market itself.

These unconventional tales show just how crazy this business is and that maintaining a wicked sense of humor might be the most effective coping mechanism unless you prefer resorting to heavy drinking.

1

The Listing that Keeps on Giving

One random Sunday morning, I received a call from a hard-money lender with whom I had collaborated on numerous occasions. While he was a decent guy, he had the reputation for charging exorbitant interest rates, even if it meant levying 20% on his own mother's property. During our conversation, he informed me about a client of his who was encountering difficulties repaying a higher-than-normal interest loan. Although late payments were not uncommon in his line of work, his level of concern regarding this particular situation was notably higher than usual.

"Yvonne, I'm calling you because you're scrappy. I know you can handle any difficult situation" he said with confidence.

He continued by explaining that his client teamed up with her now ex-boyfriend to renovate the property, aiming to flip it for profit, but their expectations fell short. Apparently, she was the one who bought the house, while her ex was supposed to act as the general contractor and handle material costs and other expenses. He portrayed himself as an experienced contractor but ended up resembling more of a glorified handyman. The completed renovations were sparse, and those that were finished were of substandard quality, as uncovered by the lender during their site inspection. To prevent defaulting on the loan, she found herself in urgent need of selling the property in its current state.

On the day of my site visit, I decided to bring a friend along to accompany me to the property as it had been unoccupied for a while, and I wanted some backup just in case. Erin was perfect for this task because she was married to a police officer, and she could serve as a reliable lookout.

As we arrived at the property and parked by the curb, my friend Erin glanced towards the house and commented, "Yvonne, you'd have to pay me to move into that dump."

"I've seen worse," I replied, unfazed. I fetched my hazmat bag from the trunk and handed gloves and masks to both of us. I tucked a small flashlight into my back pocket and kept the canister of pepper spray in my hand.

The house, a nondescript ranch-style structure, had potential, but it reminded me of the suburban home from the movie *The Burbs,* only with a gray stucco finish. If you're unfamiliar with the film, I'd recommend looking it up so you can envision exactly what we were facing.

We passed through the open gate, which seemed to be barely hanging on for dear life, held in place by just one rusty screw, maneuvering past debris scattered by overgrown bushes and trees. As we neared the front stoop, I proposed that we start by circling around the exterior first.

We stepped over plastic bags and fast-food wrappers, zig-zagged between a tipped shopping cart and a broken umbrella and came around the corner to the backyard. The scent of urine wafted through the air. A blue tarp was draped over a deck railing. Wadded sleeping bags could be seen underneath.

We stopped. "Anybody here?' No reply. Turning to Erin I said, "I'm always wary of squatters in a place that's been empty for some time, especially with owners who live out of state." We continued walking. More trash. "Watch your step."

Unfortunately, the privacy fence surrounding the back of the lot made it easier for squatters to loiter unseen. A couple of the windows on the back side of the house were shattered. One pane was broken above the latch and the window was left up wide enough for raccoons or squirrels to climb through. It led me to wonder what we would find inside.

We completed our trek around the exterior of the house. The far side mirrored the trash-scattered scene we encountered earlier, with the added surprise of a heavily stained twin-size mattress propped against the siding. It appeared as if Encino Man had made it his bed for years or that one friend who sleeps in excessive self-tanner rolled around on it. I purposefully averted my gaze, knowing that the less I saw, the fewer unsettling images my mind could imagine. The stark reality of some people enduring such foul conditions was both heart-wrenching and revolting.

As we crossed the driveway, we nudged aside the overgrown shrubbery to clear our path up the front steps.

"Here we go," I announced, turning the key in the lock.

We stepped inside. I flipped the light switch, but no light came on. The sunlight streaming in through the windows was partially blocked by the unkempt foliage outside, casting the rooms in an eerie, shadowy feel.

"Follow me," I said and took the flashlight out of my pocket. We walked through the kitchen to a door that led to the garage. I opened the electrical cabinet and flipped on the main breaker. The garage was flooded with light from three overhead fixtures. "We're good to go now."

Turning on the lights in the rooms wasn't as beneficial

as anticipated, yet it did show me a clearer perspective of the situation. Erin directed my attention to the substantial crack that spanned diagonally across the concrete garage floor.

In the kitchen, the stove sat about a foot out from the wall. Behind it, the wall was blackened with smeared soot.

"Looks like an electrical fire. Probably the boyfriend's handiwork. "At least they had an extinguisher."

Just off the family room, a doorway opened to a large empty bedroom with trash scattered across the floor. "According to the lender, this additional primary suite was built without a permit. Something a buyer will have to deal with."

As we made our way through the house, stopping to listen for movement or voices, we came across a couple more mattresses on the floors, bags of clothes, trash heaps, and a plastic bin filled with cans of food, ramen packets, and a box of Cheerios. A makeshift candle-powered stove sat on the floor below a window.

"That looks dangerous. Another fire waiting to happen," Erin said.

"I'm hoping to sell this place before it burns down. I'll have to notify the authorities again that the squatters are back. The owner said she's called them before when they saw evidence of trespassers. It's a never-ending battle."

I opened a closet door. There was an unmistakable scurrying of cockroaches. "Not good," I said, thinking to myself, *Why did I agree to list this house?*

"You ought to consider hiring an exterminator," Erin suggested, gesturing towards the sizable webs clinging to the curtain rods.

"I had hoped the spiders would take care of the roaches," I joked. If only things could work out that way.

Back outside, we walked to the curb and looked back at the sad house.

"It does have potential, don't you think?"

"If you ask me, my bet is it's never going to sell."

"Never say never," I replied. "The trick is finding the right buyer. It only takes one, one with a big imagination and lots of money."

We both laughed.

Acting on behalf of the owner, I contacted a landscaping crew to address the neglected yard and trim the overgrown shrubs. The local cleaning crews needed to remove the mattresses and other debris left by the squatters were fully booked for weeks. but a dumpster was available. Dressed in my hazmat gear, I proceeded to fill it with trash. Among the litter were used diapers, food containers crawling with maggots, used condoms, and other unsavory items.

Once again, I found myself questioning my actions. Why am I doing this? Ah, yes, because I'm scrappy and genuinely care about my clients. Fortunately, the landscapers assisted me in disposing of the mattresses into the dumpster. They also loaned me their shovel to handle the particularly repulsive items that I couldn't bring myself to touch, even with gloves on.

Additionally, I had the broken windows repaired and set up an ionizer to get rid of the noxious odors inside. With all the necessary clean up, the property was finally ready for photographs and final preparations for sale.

The new listing remained stagnant for a couple of weeks

without any activity. Caught up in my own affairs, I hadn't found the time to swing by and inspect it.

Then, a buyer's agent reached out to me. "Yvonne, I refuse to enter that property. It's surrounded by litter, and I suspect there's someone lurking inside."

"Thank you for reaching out. I'll investigate and keep you informed," I assured her.

I contacted the police, and they accompanied me to the property. No one was found inside, but the back window had been shattered once more, and the floors were sprinkled with additional debris. After the police departed, I informed my client of the situation and urged her to install an alarm, but she didn't want to invest any more money in the property. I fetched a trash bag and gloves from my car, taking it upon myself to tidy up the property, all the while pondering, *What's next with this place?*

A couple of days later, I got a call from a man looking for an investment property, any condition. *This could be the one!* I took his information and we set up a showing at the property for the next afternoon. He was scouting properties for his employer, Gerald Roth, a tech whiz of some kind. *Never heard of him.*

Arriving at the house early, I conducted a quick walk-through. There were no indications that the squatters had returned, and the duct tape placed on the broken window seemed to be holding up nicely.

A few minutes later, a black Range Rover pulled into the driveway.

As I approached, a tall, muscular 40ish man emerged from the driver's side.

"Winston," he said, nodding. "I don't have a lot of time." He handed me his card. T. Winston, Personal Assistant to Gerald Roth.

"Okay, Mr. Winston," I replied, sliding the card into my pocket. "Let's get to it." Guiding him up the steps, all the while praising the virtues of the property and all its potential.

He took video from the start of the tour to the end, but barely said a word for the entire showing. I tried to watch his expression as I revealed another obvious flaw. No emotion. None.

"Thank you so much. My employer will view this. I think he will be pleased. You might as well write up the contract."

Once back to my office, I got to work on the contract. I was just about finished with the contract when the phone rang. It was Mr. Winston.

"Mr. Roth does not want the property. Thank you for your time."

I was about to ask what caused him to reject the property when I heard the distinctive end-of-call click. I consoled myself by repeating if-it's-too-good-to-be-true-it-probably-is and berating myself. I should have known better.

The following day, a massive storm swept through, resulting in one of the large backyard trees toppling over. With astonishing accuracy, it grazed the back corner of the roof. Fortunately, one of the neighbors called to inform me of the damage.

As I hung up the phone with the kind neighbor, I thought to myself, *A f&*#ing tree! What next?*

There were no severe water leaks, but a portion of the tree obstructed the busy street below. The city issued a warning of potential fines, immediate action was necessary. I promptly notified the seller, who coordinated the removal this time while I arranged for the roofing company to assess the damage. Within just a few days, everything was resolved amidst the considerable chaos and cleanup.

Days later, I received a message from Dan Davis, interested in distressed properties. The name was not one I had worked with before, but somehow it sounded familiar. A quick social media search yielded a dozen Dan Davises. Chances are, the one I was looking for was not living in Bogota or sitting in front of a rundown trailer in Mississippi. There was one that looked promising. Owner of Davis Construction. Now I remember seeing their billboard ads. And the number he called from matched the company number.

I clicked on his profile. Fifty-ish, good-looking, graying temples.

A female voice answered the phone. "Davis Construction. How may I help you today?"

My detective work was spot on. I always like knowing a little about prospective clients before getting too involved.

"I'm returning a call from Mr. Davis regarding the purchase of distressed properties."

"One moment."

She connected me to Mr. Davis. "Call me Dan," he insisted.

We chatted for a few minutes. I described the listing, flaws and all. He did not seem deterred in the least. In fact, the more problems I mentioned, the more he wanted to see it. "How about tomorrow morning?"

Arranged.

The walk-through was brief. I could tell he knew exactly what he was looking at in terms of renovation. A smile crept across his face as I passed him the ten-page list of seller property disclosures. I half expected him to reconsider after reading everything, but instead, he glanced up and declared, "I'm ready to make an offer."

The remainder was smooth sailing, not a squatter in sight. With the offer accepted, closing completed, and a satisfied lender with a successful loan payoff, all fell into place effortlessly. The seller breathed a sigh of relief, finally liberated from her lingering nightmare and my job was officially done!

Dan completed the remodel and was so enamored with it that he decided to make it his primary residence. Occasionally, as I drive by the property, it brings me a sense of satisfaction knowing that my diligent efforts have paid off and that a deserving individual like Dan is now appreciating the space.

From a dump to desirable.

MENTAL NOTE:
Never give up, never surrender!

2

Mr. Hot Pants

Having multiple rental listings in a nearby golf community has allowed me to build relationships with many property owners and renters. As a result, I frequently receive calls from referrals.

The male voice on the phone seemed pleasant enough. "Yvonne? I received your name from one of your clients, Steven something, I forgot his last name. He said you handle rentals in the golf community."

The voice paused, so I spoke. "Yes, I do. Are you interested in leasing one of the furnished villas?"

"Very."

"Great, Mr.?" I trailed off, hoping he'd give his name.

"Gary Parsons."

We conversed briefly to determine his requirements. Once I had a clear understanding of what he was looking for, we scheduled a meeting at one of the available rental properties for the following afternoon. He mentioned he was staying at the hotel adjacent to the golf community.

The following day, I slipped into my favorite black blazer with matching slacks, grabbed my keys, and made my way to the villas, conveniently located just a quick 3-minute drive from my home.

I prefer to arrive at the property before the prospective client, allowing me to conduct a brief walkthrough. However, upon my arrival, I found Gary already waiting on the front walk. His bright green Hawaiian shirt seemed stretched to its limits, and I feared a button might pop at any moment. A belt would have been beneficial to keep his cargo shorts from sagging, as he continually hiked them up while we walked. I made a conscious effort to avoid looking down at his feet, with hairy toes peeking out from under his sandals, accompanied by long toenails. Instead, I maintained my focus on his face whenever he spoke, although it wasn't frequent. His round face was framed by a mass of thick, curly black hair. Dark sunglasses shielded his eyes, and a straw bolo-style hat on his head, leaving me to wonder if he might be bald underneath it.

We walked through the unit, one of three in the one-story building. He left his sunglasses on the entire walk-through. *Odd.* I sensed a strange vibe from him, but I reminded myself not to judge a book by its cover. The three patios were separated by privacy walls. This outer unit had a small grass lawn next to the large concrete patio and two shoulder-high shrubs before the next property. I pointed out the amenities and the community services available, including access to the golf course just down the sloping back lawn. The patio looked out over the golf course's seventh hole. That seemed to impress him. He nodded quite often, but I couldn't tell if they were positive nods or polite nods.

"Thank you for showing this to me. Quite nice," he said. "I'll be sending you my lease application tomorrow."

"Wonderful." I handed him my card. "If you have any questions, feel free to reach out."

"Sounds good, thanks. I've booked an Uber for three o'clock." He looked at his watch. "In the meantime, I think I'll walk around the neighborhood. Get a feel for the place."

He set off down the street, so I drove away.

There was no email or call from Gary the next day nor for the several days after. Occupied with other clients, I barely spared him more than a passing thought. Perhaps he encountered financial difficulties or found another rental elsewhere. Such occurrences were not uncommon; prospective tenants often proved to be unreliable.

My phone rang.

"Hello, Yvonne speaking."

"Yvonne, this is Helen."

I remembered her from last year when she moved into the golf community after her husband passed away.

"Hi, Helen? What can I do for you?"

"I know you are the rental agent for the units at Long Drive. Well, I was in my backyard and looked across the lawns. You won't believe this, but there is a naked man on the patio of fifty-seven. Walking around in his altogether. And quite frankly, he's not the kind of naked man you'd want to see. Whoever you rented that to needs to be spoken to ASAP."

"Helen, I haven't rented out that property. Are you sure?"

"I know a naked man when I see one!" she protested.

"I meant, are you sure it was at fifty-seven?"

"Oh, yes. No mistake. If I see him again, do you want me to get a photo?"

"That won't be necessary," I assured her. "I will look into this."

As soon as we finished, I called the unit owner to be sure he had not let anyone stay at his condo. Unfortunately, now he is worried.

I drove over to the condo, then decided to pull up past it to stop at Helen's building first and get a look at the situation from a distance. From Helen's description, I thought it would be a good idea.

Helen greeted me and pulled me into her front hall.

Her eyes were bulging. "I didn't expect you so soon, Yvonne. Did you see him?"

"I just arrived, Helen. I thought you and I could have a look from your place first."

She led me through her spotless living room and dining room out to the patio. She had the center unit in this building which made me wonder how she saw the man in the first place.

"Muffin," she called. A little French poodle tottered over to her from the shade of a lounge chair, tail wagging. "Let's play in the grass." She clipped a long leash onto his collar.

We walked off the concrete patio onto the lawn and watched Muffin run around.

"He's there," Helen whispered. "Don't look. Well, look but don't look like you are looking."

"Is he still naked?" I asked.

"No," she giggled. "He's napping on a lounge chair."

"Thank goodness for that," I said, breathing a sigh of relief. I glanced over. Except for the dark blue 80s-short shorts, he was naked. His well-rounded belly and chest were covered in dark hair. His pale skin had a reddish hue. *Too much sun too soon.* I wracked my brain. Something about him seemed familiar.

"Well," asked Helen in a conspiratorial whisper, "what are you going to do about it?"

"First, let me get a photo for proof. I'll pretend Muffin is my subject." I pulled out my phone and stood with Muffin between me and Mr. Hot Pants. I was able to get a few shots before Muffin started barking at a golfer off in the distance.

Out of the corner of my eye, I saw Mr. Hot Pants stand, stretch, and pull the lounge closer to the patio doors out of our line of sight. As he walked, I remembered that gait. *It's Gary! What the –*

"I know who it is, Helen." I waved to her to bring Muffin onto her patio. "I showed him the unit a few days ago. His name is Gary if that's even his real name. I need to notify the police since the unit owner made it clear he didn't let anyone stay there."

"Do you think he's living there illegally?" asked Helen.

"It appears so. Did you happen to notice if there are lights on in the evening?"

"Didn't notice. Sorry."

"That's OK. If you hadn't called, I wouldn't have even known about him."

"Well, now that I know about him, I'm staying inside."

"A good idea. Muffin too, I think." Muffin wagged his tail at the mention of his name. Helen pulled a treat from her pocket and tossed it to him. "I'll keep you posted."

"Be careful, Yvonne." Helen patted my hand.

I left Helen at her front door and walked to my car to make calls. I glanced back at fifty-seven and locked my car doors.

A movement in the rearview mirror caught my eye. I instinctively slunk down in my seat, keeping my eyes on the mirror. There was Mr. Hot Pants, walking around the side of the condo towards the curb, sporting yet another Hawaiian shirt, a straw hat, and sunglasses. With a leather bag slung over one shoulder, he resembled someone who had won a cruise ship tour but never actually embarked on the journey.

I couldn't turn on the car and drive away without attracting his attention, so I waited. He walked back to the shade of the front stoop. I inched my body around in the seat to look over my shoulder. He was staring right at my car. I prayed the tinted windows did their job. *Does he recognize the car?*

A couple of minutes later, an older Camry pulled up and he got in. As it passed me, I could see the Uber sticker in the rear window.

I called the condo owner immediately to confirm Gary was attempting to squat.

I reached into my glove compartment and grabbed my pepper spray. I got out of the car and retraced Gary's steps to the back patio. As I approached the corner, I stopped and aimed my spray in case Gary had not been alone. I stepped onto the patio. *Nobody. Whew!*

Under the awning on the patio, there were several computer screens and electronics. Empty plastic water bottles and various empty alcoholic beverage bottles were strewn about, and several suitcases stood against the patio's glass door. I checked. The door was locked. The inside of the house did not look any different than when I was last here, so I hoped he hadn't been inside.

I stepped back to the edge of the patio to get photos. I wanted to get out of there as soon as possible.

"What a mess," a voice behind me said.

After I climbed back into my skin, I realized the voice belonged to Helen. "You gave me a scare!"

"Sorry. When I saw you get out of your car after the man left, I worried."

"I'm going to call the police. Can I give them your name? They'll probably want to ask questions."

"Sure. And I can give a *complete* description," Helen said, blushing. She continued to laugh as she walked Muffin back to her condo.

The police stakeout was unsuccessful. Officer Kelsey filled me in. When "Gary" didn't return after several hours, they collected the suitcases, computer monitors, and other items. I put the lounge chairs inside the unit and locked everything up.

A couple of days later, Officer Kelsey reached out to me once more. The fingerprints found on the suitcases belonged to a man wanted in three states for fraud and theft. They had apprehended a suspect, and now they wanted *me* to identify him. What on earth? – I'm just trying to rent an apartment!

I called Helen to let her know and added, "This morning, I have to go to the station and pick him out of a line-up. I hope I can identify him; He had a hat and sunglasses on when I saw him up close."

"I could identify him in his altogether from a distance," Helen offered.

"I don't think the other men in the line-up would be too eager to help out with that."

"Perhaps not."

On the way to the station, I tried to imagine what the line-up experience would be like. My only references were police shows on TV with one-way mirrors and darkened rooms.

Once there, the line-up identification was harder than I

thought it would be. Two of the men looked very similar, but I did remember that "Gary" had a thick neck, similar to that one guy on the 90-Day Fiancé show. Thanks to that clue, I was able to pinpoint who Gary was.

Officer Kelsey said with my I.D. and the matching fingerprints, they could charge him and notify the other jurisdictions he was wanted in.

I was so glad the whole episode was over.

Surprise. Eight days later, I got a text from "Gary" wanting me to return his belongings from the condo. He claimed a friend had dropped them off thinking it was his new rental. What a weird thing to lie about.

I contacted the police department to inquire about Gary's status, but they couldn't disclose his legal name or whereabouts. Opting to disregard his texts, they eventually stopped. Gary probably realized that the authorities had confiscated his stolen goods. I blocked his burner phone number and never crossed paths with him again. Thankfully, Villa Fifty-Seven found a wonderful tenant who happened to be one of the police officers who had been part of the stakeout.

MENTAL NOTE:
Sometimes the cover is the book.

3

I'm a Good Christian Woman!

Selling a luxury listing can present its challenges. Karen, a prospective buyer, was acting as her own agent, which typically simplifies the transaction. However, things don't always go according to plan.

As we strolled through my exquisitely decorated listing, Karen struggled to contain her excitement despite her efforts to stay cool. During our earlier phone conversation that day, she expressed her disappointment with the houses she had previously viewed which failed to meet her expectations. Evidently, my client's house checked all the right boxes for her. Throughout the tour, Karen asked all the pertinent questions and showered the property with compliments.

"The dining room and kitchen are even larger than I envisioned from the photos online," Karen said. "Better for entertaining."

"And the great room is large enough to accommodate separate areas for guests to mingle," I added.

She nodded. "Love the cathedral ceiling." I could tell by the way her eyes darted around that she was imagining how she would furnish the room.

The property was located in an up-scale gated neighborhood, each home unique in style and layout, but all featuring an attached three-car garage, paver driveway, and an oversized manicured lawn on a large lot with mature trees separating each property. The homes were set back from the sidewalks and street, so road noise was minimal.

"You mentioned an HOA?" Karen asked.

"The seller has had no problems with the HOA in the years she has lived here. In fact, she said she pays her dues and they do what they say they'll do. No complaints or issues."

"Good to know. In some places, they are a nightmare," Karen said, rolling her eyes.

"I'm sure we both could tell some stories," I said. We had a good laugh.

I was relieved when she said, "This is the house."

"Great, draw up the contract and I'll present it to my clients," I said.

Upon returning to my office, I immediately dialed my client, Gina, to deliver the good news. She happily accepted Karen's clean offer. *We were on our way.*

Karen remained in contact over the following couple of weeks, consistently cheerful and friendly, even as she posed questions about the property. The inspection proceeded without any red flags, making for smooth sailing. Meanwhile, my sellers were in the process of purchasing two homes, contingent on the sale of their primary residence. Fortunately, both transactions were progressing nicely despite the numerous moving parts, thanks to the fantastic cooperation of the listing agents involved.

As closing day for my client's primary home approached, things took a sudden turn. It was as if a switch had been flipped. Karen went from sweet to sour, sourer than expired milk on a scorching day.

I received a long rambling email from Karen. First, she claimed my escrow officer was rude, questioning the legitimacy of her cashier's check for the down payment, which I found hard to believe. She also doubted the escrow officer's ability to close the file on time. I happen to know the escrow officer has over twenty years of experience and have worked with her on several occasions. Always the model of professionalism. I need to give her a call and find out what transpired. If Karen carried on with her like she had in her email to me, I could see her cutting Karen short. I suppose that could be interpreted as rude, but well-deserved, nonetheless.

I responded, assuring Karen that I had faith in the escrow officer to do an excellent job as usual. Her lack of response led me to believe she was satisfied.

On the day before the closing, I met Karen and her reserved husband at the property for the walkthrough. The husband seemed almost invisible, making it evident who wore the pants in their relationship. Karen was polite, but the easy banter we had during the previous weeks was gone. My client and her family were filling three twelve-foot pods that sat in the driveway. It looked like they still had quite a bit to pack up.

"My client assured me that they would be out by closing tomorrow." I said as we walked towards the front entrance.

"They'd better be," muttered Karen to me under her breath.

I just looked at her. *What happened to that easy-going person I had spent the last month with?* I had to resist the urge to roll my eyes so intensely that my retinas threatened to detach.

"See you tomorrow," Karen said with no emotion. As she walked out the door, her husband trailed behind like the last in a line of scurrying chicks crossing a street. I observed their hurried departure before returning to assist my client with moving some boxes. After that awkward moment, I made a conscious effort to shift my focus back to the positive aspects of the situation.

On the morning of closing day, my phone rang. It was my client. *Think positive,* I told myself before answering. "Hi, Gina. Everything OK?"

"Well, Yvonne, the Pod company called. Their truck broke down, they will be three hours late getting here. I hope that is not going to be a problem."

My mind swirled with the possibilities Karen could come up with to make it a problem. I couldn't saddle my client with that. "I don't think it will be a huge problem. I'll let the buyer know, though. Otherwise, you're good to go?"

"Yes, we'll be finished packing soon. Thank you so much."

As soon as I was off the phone, I dashed off a quick email to Karen. The fewer surprises at closing, the better.

No response.

About forty minutes later, I received an email from the HOA asking for an estimated time the pods would be removed. Instead of responding by email, I called the number they provided.

Apparently, Karen had called and emailed HOA management several times demanding they investigate the pods situation and what their by-laws say about pods in driveways. She was not making friends with the HOA. I could tell from the description of their interactions. I couldn't help but think, *Do you really want to upset your HOA before you even move in?* It would be Karen's problem after today.

Later that morning, the property was recorded with the tax assessor, and Karen went directly to the home.

Less than thirty minutes later, my phone rang; it was Gina, the seller.

"Yvonne, the buyer is here at the house. My boys and I are loading their bikes from the garage into the pods and this Karen is screaming at us, 'Post possession, Post possession, Get off my property!' and accusing us of violating the contract."

I could hear Karen's high-pitched ranting in the background. I couldn't help but think, *Who yells in front of children like that?*

"First things first," I said. "Gina, are all of your possessions out of the house?"

"Now, yes. I let the boys keep their bikes out to ride since the pod truck won't be here for a while, but we took a break for a snack, and they put them in the garage. Karen went ballistic when she saw the bikes in the garage."

I did not understand what Karen's issue was. Gina and her family would be history in an hour. Why the drama?

"Hang in there, Gina. I'll see what I can do."

No sooner had I hung up with Gina, than my cell rang again. It was Karen. I put on my cheeriest voice. "Hi, Karen. Everything good with your new home?"

I put the phone on speaker, set it on my desk to save my hearing, and let Karen unload. I wasn't going to let her know I had just spoken to Gina or that I knew where she was.

"Did you know *your people* are still at *my* house?" she barked.

"If the pod truck hasn't arrived, I imagine they are, but they will be gone soon. My client mentioned the pod truck broke down, sorry for the delay! I did let you know that was a possibility."

"Well, I'm taking pictures of everything, and you'll be responsible for any damages I find. And I don't like the fact that you are playing games with me. I'm no amateur you can pull one over on. I'm a good Christian woman, but you are making me behave in ungodly ways. I'm going to report you to your broker and the Association!"

"You do what you think is best," I replied, not wanting to escalate the situation.

"I will," she snapped. The call abruptly ended, leaving me to reflect on the swift dismissal. It struck me how effortlessly she ended it, likely fueled by the immense frustration I had unwittingly provoked.

Karen claiming to not be an amateur got me thinking. *What agent behaves like this?* I opened my laptop and checked Karen's production numbers to see what an expert she was. Only one sale, one sale in the past five years. And that was her personal purchase. *Some expert. More like 100% amateur.*

Gina called again. "The pod truck arrived. Karen had to move her car out of the way, so she drove off."

"I'll be right over. I want to get pictures before Karen returns. At this point, I really don't trust her not to blame you or your boys for anything."

"I'll get some photos too," Gina offered.

"Great, and apologize to your boys for their getting caught up in this."

"I already told them it's a great life lesson about how not to deal with people."

"Good for you. Oh, if Karen comes back before I get there, text me."

"Sure thing."

I grabbed my stuff and rushed out.

When I arrived, Gina and her boys were sitting in the air-conditioned comfort of her car. Gina hopped out and greeted me as I opened my car door.

"No Karen," Gina said.

"I'll make this quick, but you don't have to stick around. If Karen comes back, it would be better if you've vacated the premises. Good thing your new home is all set and the seller let you do a pre-possession for a day."

"Absolutely!" Gina raised her hands and yelled, "Post possession! Post possession!" mocking Karen's earlier conniption.

I waved to the boys as Gina returned to her car.

As soon as they pulled out, I got to work. I took photos of the driveway where the pods had been, and the rest of the driveway for good measure. No damage, not a single scratch. I walked around the outside of the house getting shots from many angles, removed my lockbox and confirmed with the sign company that the post will definitely be removed the following day if not today.

Later that afternoon, I got an agitated voice message from Karen. The gate transponder was missing, and I'd better get it to her or she'll add that to her negative report. I called Gina immediately.

"So sorry, Yvonne."

"Don't worry, just get it over there as soon as you can."

My phone rang a few minutes later. It was Gina. My heart raced, *What now?*

"Yvonne, I just had the most bizarre interaction with Karen. I rang the doorbell. Karen answered. I was expecting a screaming maniac like earlier, but she was sweet as pie, saying they love the home and God bless you. She even gave me a hug. I'm thinking a little while ago you were yelling at me and my kids to get off your property and threatening to sue me, now this? I think there may be some medications involved."

"I was thinking that very thing," I said, and we laughed. "At least it's over."

I was wrong. I received another voice mail from Karen. "Stop playing games! Give me the mailbox key!" Her voice sounded like the exorcist's.

Again, I called Gina.

"My ex must have it; I'll have him drop it off tomorrow. Is that OK?"

"No, I'd rather take care of this now. Is he still staying at that resort down the street? I could pick it up right now."

"Yes. I'll let him know you're on your way."

I swung by Gina's ex's, got the key, and stopped to pick up a cheap colorful bouquet of assorted flowers and a greeting card. On the card, I wrote *Congratulations and Thank you!* and put the key in the envelope with it. On the sealed envelope I wrote *God Bless!*

I pulled into Karen's driveway, left the flowers and envelope on the front doorstep, and slipped away before anyone noticed. I literally sprinted away like a child who had just placed a paper bag filled with dog poop on the doorstep and lit it on fire.

When I stopped at the end of the street, I pulled out my phone and texted her, *The mailbox key is on your doorstep.*

No response or thank you.

After taking a deep breath, I set out on my way. However, the following day, I made the decision to block her number because the transaction was officially over.

I don't want to give the Devil's Mistress too much credit, but this woman/agent had been infiltrating my dreams; her presence felt toxic and inexplicably unsettling. *Have you ever met someone whose gaze sends chills down your spine in a profoundly disturbing way?* This newfound side of Karen was weird. Typically, I don't allow others to affect me like this.

My client and I agreed that reporting Karen to her broker would be pointless, as she doesn't really sell anything and appeared to possess the volatility reminiscent of the main character from *Fatal Attraction*.

Bye Felicia!

MENTAL NOTE:
Take this medication by mouth as directed by your doctor, usually once daily in the morning.

4

Do You Like Tigers?

As the listing agent, I had the privilege of representing a recently constructed, luxurious residence spanning 10,000 square feet. Nestled on a multi-acre lot just beyond the town limits, the exorbitant home was strategically perched on a hillside, offering breathtaking panoramic views. The layout was a sought-after design, featuring six bedrooms, five and a half bathrooms, an expansive kitchen, a formal dining area, and a generously sized living room with soaring twenty-five-foot ceilings. Within the main living quarters, an awe-dropping glass-encased, temperature-controlled wine storage, capable of accommodating 1000 bottles, served as a striking focal point, elevating the space with its sophistication. The primary bedroom exuded contemporary charm with its edgy black walls and commanding spike chandelier over the Wyoming king bed setting a distinct tone of extra.

And let's not forget the elevator, resort-style negative-edge pool, six-car garage, separate guesthouse, and a large, meticulously manicured lawn.

Inside the property, there was also a private bar/lounge and a gym with accordion doors that opened seamlessly to the pool area. These details I included in the listing brochure, I could go on and on. This property resonated deeply with my personal tastes to the extent that I found myself wanting to move in immediately! With its modern flair and extravagant amenities, I couldn't help but envision the ideal buyer as a crypto millionaire or a famous influencer. This home exuded an undeniable allure that was sure to captivate anyone seeking a property that embodies contemporary elegance and status. My client's impeccable taste was evident; this property was a page straight out of *Luxe Interiors + Design* magazine.

As I rode the elevator down to the basement for the first time, I couldn't help but wonder what awaited me beyond the doors. In this line of work, you never know. The elevator walls were covered with Gucci tiger head print wallpaper with its dozens of staring eyes and gaping, fanged mouths.

Once listed on the market, we received an influx of showings. Open house guests ranging from young families to noisy neighbors and relocation business professionals. Visitors couldn't help but comment on the tiger wallpaper. However, it didn't appear to significantly sway their decision—it was more of a curious observation than a decisive factor in making an offer.

During one open house event, a young woman with long blonde hair arrived early and patiently waited outside. Though I hadn't yet opened the door to visitors, I caught a glimpse of her through the bay window. She was dressed as though she were headed to a Miami after-hours party, sporting a short, red, fitted dress, and her makeup looked professionally done.

"Hello, I'm Yvonne," I introduced myself as I opened the door and held back my judgy face. "Are you here for the open house?"

"Yes, hi. I'm Sandy," she replied, handing me her card. "I know I'm early. I'm waiting for my client."

"Come up on the step in the shade," I invited her, extending my hand to shake hers. "I'll leave you to get situated," I added, making my way back into the house just as a dated Maserati pulled into the circular drive, catching Sandy's attention.

Shortly after, they entered the house and introductions were made. She introduced him only as Joel. He stood about six feet tall with a modestly muscular physique, accented with a bit of a beer belly. He gave the impression of someone in their late fifties and sported a deep tan that hinted at a history of major sun exposure, perhaps coupled with a habit of smoking. A sense of familiarity washed over me; I could have sworn I saw this man before.

As I walked them around, I tried to picture him at a previous showing somewhere, but nothing clicked. That voice, that self-assured laugh, they seemed so familiar. I thought that maybe I had seen him on television.

I showed them the main floor and back patio. Joel was impressed by the large inground pool and lounge. Sandy gave me a thumbs-up behind his back.

Back inside, Joel's eyes lit up when the elevator doors opened to reveal the tiger print. He laughed out loud for a good thirty seconds and took out his phone to take a photo.

I asked him, "Do you like tigers?"

"Yes," he replied with a crooked smirk.

After we finished touring around, the three of us stood at the front door as more visitors arrived and walked toward us.

Joel turned to me. "Are you the listing agent?" he asked, handing me his card.

"Yes," I answered, but I wondered why he would be asking me that when he was there with his buyer agent, plus he gave me his business card. I had questions.

I watched as he and Sandy shook hands and said their

goodbyes. Joel turned to me and waved as he got into his sports car.

Later that afternoon when there was a break in visitors, I retrieved Joel's card and decided to Google his name. To my surprise, it appeared that Joel might be the present owner of a well-known wildlife sanctuary and renowned circus ringmaster, showcased on reality television programs. It crossed my mind that he fit right in; his eccentricity matched the property perfectly. However, further findings revealed a less savory side to his reputation. Reports suggested he had a history of petty criminal activities and deceitful behavior, including a lawsuit filed against him by well-known artists for allegedly infringing on trademarks. He had also been found guilty of federal mail fraud, among other offenses. Clearly, not the type of individual I wanted to grant access to my client's home.

Holding Sandy's paper-thin business card in hand, I couldn't shake the feeling that she likely hadn't vetted this individual thoroughly. With doubts creeping in, I decided to give her a call.

"Sandy, how did you meet your client, Joel?"

"He saw my information on Zillow and called me. I just met him."

"Did you check if he was qualified for this price point?"

"Not yet. He wanted to see the house this morning, so it was kind of a rush. To be honest, I'm hoping to land a luxury sale to boost my career," Sandy explained.

"There's nothing wrong with that," I assured her. "We all have to start somewhere." I refrained from mentioning how meeting a stranger off the internet without researching them seemed careless, but that was just my cautious nature, not to mention common sense. I couldn't help but wonder if Joel had chosen her because she looked attractive or because of her expertise as an agent. While we conversed, I discreetly looked up her production and discovered she had no previous sales on record. I had to assume he chose her because of her appearance.

After that encounter, I never heard from Sandy again. I half expected a call from Joel attempting to make an offer directly, but none came. I wasn't inclined to reach out to him either. However, I was certain it wasn't the tiger print wallpaper that scared him away.

The property ended up being purchased by one of the first couples who viewed it when we initially hit the market. They had plans to travel to France for a month and decided that if the property was still available upon their return, they would buy it. Being avid wine collectors and enthusiastic entertainers, the place was ideal for them, plus they loved the edgy décor, tigers and all. Timing aligned perfectly, and the home found its rightful owners. It's funny to think that a retired couple from Minnesota would be the ones to claim it.

MENTAL NOTE:
Expect the unexpected.

5

My House Is Perfect

"**T**his place is wonderful, Yvonne," Sheila gushed as we stood in front of the two-story home. Its stucco exterior, arched doorways, and brick-red tile roof gave it a classic southwestern motif. The pea gravel accents along the concrete driveway and front walk added a nice touch. *The power of curb appeal,* I thought. Sheila's husband showed less enthusiasm but seemed pleased his wife was happy.

The front door opened into a spacious and airy cathedral-ceiling entryway with a tile mosaic floor.

"Just beautiful," Sheila said. She had not been as impressed at any of the other properties we toured. "I hope the rest of the house doesn't disappoint."

I tried to manage expectations. "According to the listing, it needs a few light cosmetic fixups, which is understandable given the property is about twenty years old."

"Of course," Sheila replied. Her husband shrugged in agreement.

As we strolled through the expansive living areas, we reached the sizable dining room. "The current owner occupies the house, and the furniture you see can be included in the sale if we agree on a price," I explained to them. Personally, the furniture struck me as outdated and bulky, particularly the travertine coffee table, which I estimated weighed a hefty 500 pounds. Interestingly, despite the owner/agent's claim in the listing notes that the furniture was like-new and available for

sale, it seemed more like new in 1990.

From the looks of it, the kitchen appliances had been updated recently. I couldn't tell if Sheila or her husband could smell the lavender-scented Glade plug-ins, but I noticed right away. It's usually a sign that the seller is masking an unpleasant odor of some kind. Cigarettes? Mold? Cat urine? I couldn't detect anything specific.

"Oh my, a pizza oven," Sheila said, laughing. "That will get some use." She opened and closed the oven door.

The primary bedroom and ensuite even got a nod from her husband. Upstairs had two more bedrooms, a full bath, and a work/hobby room. The heat on this level was stifling and I apologized for the lack of air conditioning. "The owner is trying to save money, I imagine, since he's not home at the moment. I could turn it on for you." They both shook their heads.

I finally saw a big smile on the husband's face when we walked out onto the deck, and he saw the inground pool. "Nice," he said. "I could use that right now."

"The patio is big enough to host barbecues," I pointed out. "And the pergola limits the afternoon sun."

"The asking price is in our range, dear, what do you think? Should we put in an offer?" Sheila looked at her husband with raised eyebrows.

"I'll let you two discuss it," I said and went back into the house to let them have a private conversation. I took the time alone to check the air filter in the hallway air return. As I suspected, black and packed with dust, probably not changed in twenty years. If my clients want the property, the home inspector will point this out.

After a few minutes, they came in and were ready to make an offer.

I called Brandon, the property owner and also listing agent. He was cheerful and, in retrospect, a little too eager to get the contract signed and the sale completed.

"We'll have an inspector there as soon as possible," I assured him. There was a pause.

"Great," he replied. "I'm sure it will go splendidly."

I thought, who says splendidly anymore?

I drew up the contract, had it signed by my clients, and sent it off to Brandon.

I called around to my usual inspectors. Ed, who had an impeccable record for being thorough, had a cancellation and could fit us in the next afternoon. *Sometimes you get lucky.*

Regrettably, Ed's inspection report uncovered numerous significant repairs necessary. The original roof exhibited multiple cracked tiles, warranting a complete replacement. An active leak was detected in the laundry room ceiling. Additionally, a piece of exposed rebar in the pool posed a potential safety risk. Particularly concerning was the malfunctioning air conditioning system, deemed irreparable and requiring replacement. Accessing the attic was challenging, as it was obstructed by stored items in an upstairs closet, likely an attempt to deter inspection. Fortunately, Ed managed to access the attic through the garage and discovered an abandoned HVAC unit, which, if removed and replaced, would incur substantial expenses.

I let my buyer know Ed's findings and we reviewed the report together.

"What can we do about all of that?" Sheila inquired.

"Pick items you would like repaired mentioned in the inspection report and I'll draw up the BINSR, that's a Buyer Inspection Notice Seller Response. That will give the seller five days to say whether he will make the repairs or give a credit."

"And if he doesn't?"

"Then the ball is in your court. You can negotiate a lower price or walk away."

"Ugh. I'll let my husband know."

My buyer's requested repairs included a new roof and replacement of the air conditioning system. Considering that my clients were paying top dollar for this property in a competitive market, their expectations were aligned with those of homes commanding similar prices, which typically include functioning air conditioning and solid roofs without leaks.

I sent off the BINSR and inspection report to Brandon. Not ten minutes later, my phone rang. Brandon was not pleased.

Skip the niceties. Brandon started on a rant. "That roof was perfectly fine. Your inspector must have broken the tiles when he walked on the roof to inspect. How much does he weigh anyway? I might just sue him for damages." Little did he know, Ed inspected the roof using a drone.

Before I could respond, Brandon continued, "And that exposed rebar at the bottom of the pool is just a rust stain left by a penny someone had dropped. Did your inspector go for a swim? I doubt it. And the AC? That works perfectly fine as well. Your inspector must have been in a big rush. He didn't allow time for the system to cool down. It's a big house, you know. Where did you find this guy? How much are you paying him?" Brandon's voice kept getting higher and higher as he spoke. I

was afraid he'd burst a blood vessel if he kept going.

"Brandon," I said in a calm voice when he paused, "I have used this inspector many times before. He's one of the best."

"He helps you make deals, you mean? Finding non-existent problems."

I ignored the accusation and assumed he was smoking crack. "Brandon, we will expect your written response to the BINSR within the five days."

He muttered something I'm sure was derogatory, but I couldn't make it out before he hung up. It's just as well.

As anticipated, Brandon refused to address the repairs or engage in negotiations. My clients opted to cancel the deal and continue their search elsewhere. I felt a sense of relief; it was clear that we had dodged a bullet.

Brandon wasn't finished with us. I answered his call. "I'll sue you and your clients for breach of contract," he shouted into the phone. "You'll be sorry."

"Brandon, they are within their rights to cancel. You know this, being a designated broker at your own firm. And the courts will know this."

He tried to change tactics. "I'll bet you have your eye on a bigger commission with a different property. That's why you got them to change their minds."

I crumpled up a piece of paper over my phone receiver, pretending that static was interfering with the call while he spoke. Without responding, I simply ended the call. This guy was out of his mind! I was aware that we were still within the due diligence period for canceling the deal, and he had no legal grounds to pursue a lawsuit. With that, the matter was settled.

If someone believes one plus one is four, they are absolutely correct, enjoy - goodbye!

Thankfully, Sheila and her husband were enthusiastic about continuing their search for a new home. Shortly after terminating the contract with Brandon, a new property came onto the market. This home was much newer, more affordable, had exceptional views, and was situated in an area that better suited my clients' preferences. The entire transaction proceeded effortlessly with the help of the professional listing agent, and the icing on the cake was witnessing the sheer joy on my clients' faces.

I'm certain news spread quickly about Brandon's refusal to negotiate. I randomly kept an eye on the listing's status, it went under contract and fell through at least four times. Best of luck to you, Mr. "My house is perfect."

MENTAL NOTE:
Being stubborn isn't always smart.

6

Show Me the Money

Eduardo was a Mexican businessman who contacted me with an interest in purchasing a luxury home in my area. He had seen my advertisements and thought I looked like I knew what I was doing. I have no idea how he could tell that from a picture, but a possible sale is a possible sale.

"Miss Yvonne, you must show me the most wonderful homes that are for sale." His heavy accent and hesitation with some words indicated to me that English was not a strong second language for him, but he spoke well enough.

We agreed to meet the following morning to look at two properties I thought would interest him. "Muy grande," he repeated. "Big and beautiful."

"I got it, Eduardo," I assured him.

Before ending the call, I asked him for proof of funds, but he said it might take a while for his bank to provide the paperwork from Mexico City. "I don't want to miss a perfecto house," he pleaded.

Usually, I will show one or two properties before requesting proof of funds, but after that, I do not waste my time. Occasionally, I get a foreign client like Eduardo looking for a second home, a place to call home when in the U.S. This is not a problem. Aside from a little extra paperwork, the process is as smooth as it is for a domestic buyer.

I arrived at the first property just ahead of Eduardo.

When he stepped out of his car, he glanced toward the house and grinned. "Perfecto." He flashed a bright smile and clasped his hands together, nodding toward me. He was short and a little on the stout side, but well dressed in a navy-blue suit, white shirt, and tie. His jacket was open enough to reveal a delicate gold chain and crucifix.

The property was a sprawling one-story ranch house on the edge of town with a barn and small guest house. As we toured the house, Eduardo asked many questions, some of them barely relevant to a purchase.

"What do you think of this house?" he asked. "Would you live here?"

"It's too big for me," I replied.

"You live alone?" he asked.

I realized then he was digging for personal information, so I changed the subject. "What do you think of the patio?" I opened the glass door and led him to the large sandstone patio. He must have sensed my discomfort. That was the end of his questioning.

"We must see the second house before I take up your whole day, Miss."

We had spent over an hour at this property. The day was looking taken up already.

The second property was in town. It was not far from the business district in a planned upscale neighborhood. The home was a two-story Mediterranean Revival on a moderately sized lot. The neighborhood had numerous of this style as well as several Mid-Century Modern dwellings.

I tried to get a read on Eduardo's wants, but he seemed to be all over the place, fitting the stereotype of a typical guy. While I acknowledge this comment might be considered sexist, this guy was beginning to annoy me. I felt the urge to shake him, like the scene in the movie *The Notebook* and yell, "What do you want? What do you want?"

After another hour-plus of questions, Eduardo thanked me for my time and said he would be in touch.

"You are so kind, Senora Yvonne, but I have a plane to catch. I will be back to continue looking."

He took my hand as if to kiss it, but I turned it into a handshake.

"I hope to hear from your bank soon," I said. Thinking, *Seriously WTH*.

As his car pulled away, I had hopes that this would eventually lead to a sale.

I did not hear from his bank that week, and since he wasn't around, I let it go.

A few months later, Eduardo called. "Miss Yvonne, I am back to look at more casas."

"That's wonderful, Eduardo. I do need to let you know that I did not hear from your bank in Mexico City. I do need proof of funds to show you more properties."

He placed a hand on his chest. "I am a private person. I do not like sharing that kind of information."

I wondered then if he had ever even contacted his bank the last time he was here.

"I could give you the names of a couple of lenders in the area. They might be able to help you," I offered. "I'll text you their information."

"Gracias," he replied. "I think I would like to look at condos downtown. Someplace safe to leave vacant while I'm in Mexico but for to use when I'm in town."

"I know just the place," I said. "Sunset Ridge Residences."

We met at the condo complex parking lot. "This is quite different from the properties you were interested in before," I commented.

"Si, but I have new thoughts of what I want."

"That's great. We're making progress."

The condo complex was huge with a dozen or more high-rise buildings. I have shown and sold several units here in the past couple of years. Management is top tier and buyers are happy with their purchase.

I showed Eduardo three different units, both one and two bedrooms. Since they were in different locations in the complex, we spent much time walking from one to another along the tree-lined walkways between them.

"Muy bueno," Eduardo repeated as we toured the third condo. Again, the endless questions, always with a smile and careful attention to my answers.

I was feeling good that he was nearing a decision. When we went our separate ways, I reminded him to contact the lenders.

A short while later, I got a call from Dale, one of the lenders.

"Yvonne, I can't lend to this Eduardo you referred to me. He's a foreign national and has no Social Security number."

I had to admit, that meant a sale to Eduardo was looking less likely. Unless he had the cash, which he might.

Eduardo did not call after our tour, and I didn't want to press the issue of funding. I was busy with other clients.

A few months later, Eduardo called again. I was out of town, so I referred him to a different agent, one I knew was fluent in Spanish. Eduardo never called him, even after the agent reached out to him.

Another few months passed and again I referred Eduardo to the other agent. Again, he never called the agent.

One day, about a year after that, I got an email from Eduardo. "Show me something special," he wrote.

I thought back to our property tours. He didn't seem like the type to use a real estate agent to see how people had decorated their houses or tour properties to get ideas for their own building projects. I did recall that Eduardo was paying a lot of attention to me, watching me answer his questions, following around behind me. My creep meter hadn't gone off, but now I'm thinking he was never interested in buying a property. He was only ever interested in spending time with me. Well, after a couple of years dealing with this tire kicker, I'm done!

MENTAL NOTE:
Cook or get out of the kitchen!

7

Design on a Dime

At times, the home-selling process may seem uneventful, almost surreal. Smooth transactions without hitches in offers, loans, inspections, or other matters can lull one into a false sense of security. Nonetheless, I've come to expect the unexpected.

Greg, my client who I met through golf, had his sights set on a home where he could reside for a few years before flipping it for profit. With a charismatic demeanor, single and ready to mingle, Greg had recently gone through a nasty divorce and was eager to embrace his next chapter. In the brief time I spent with him, he became like the older brother I never wanted. Our home tours were filled with laughter, and his repertoire of dad jokes were bad but good, if you know what I mean.

After scouring the market, we stumbled upon a gem: a charming mid-century brick house full of potential. Complete with a quaint wrap-around deck and ample yard space, it was a promising find. Greg decided to test the waters with a low-ball offer on this single-family dwelling, and to our surprise, the owner accepted almost instantaneously, without even bothering to negotiate.

"That doesn't happen often in this market. I'm surprised his agent didn't recommend countering us," I said to Greg.

"If the owner didn't have an offer in the three weeks since we attempted to look at it the first time, maybe he feels lucky to get any offer," Greg suggested.

"Good point. The presence of the owner's son residing there may be hindering in-person viewings."

"Yeah, I'm not sure what was up with that guy. Did he even have a job?"

I mentioned, "Staying for free at Dad's property. Probably not. Let's just hope he has a place to go before the closing."

"That won't be a problem, Yvonne, will it?"

"Typically, not. I've never had that happen, plus the listing agent confirmed he would be moved out on time." In the back of my mind, I had a sudden thought. *There's a first time for everything.*

The transaction had been progressing nicely, with the owner's son, Joshua, proving to be incredibly accommodating during inspections and so on. *I guess his father had something to do with that.* However, as Greg and I arrived for the final walk-through on the hot, sunny morning of the closing day, things veered off course in a most unpredictable manner.

"What the . . ." Greg muttered.

The two police cars in the driveway were the first clue that something was very wrong. Scattered on the front lawn area were shattered remnants of several kitchen cabinets and assorted boxes. As we pulled up to the curb, we could see two uniformed officers talking with a skinny, naked, jittery young man who looked to not have shaved in a few days. Why I fixated on his unshaven face while his genitals were flailing around, I couldn't tell you. Even in that state, I knew it was the owner's son from having met him during the inspections. He was holding onto a large suitcase, waving his arms, and pacing while talking. We couldn't hear what he was saying, so I rolled down the window part way.

Only snippets of the young man's rants were audible. "No time. Wrong day. Dad said to."

I looked at Greg. "Don't worry. We'll get it straightened out."

"Promise?"

We both watched the scene. I could hear one of the officers repeating, "Just take it easy, calm down." The other officer took hold of the young man's wrists and cuffed him, hands behind his back. Thankfully, the first officer picked up a shirt from the lawn and tied it around the man to conceal his parts.

"He's definitely on something," Greg said, "and I don't mean coffee."

"I'm glad you have a sense of humor about this," I said.

"Not really. Why are the kitchen cabinets on the lawn, anyway? Aren't they supposed to be part of the kitchen?"

"I have no idea why there are cabinets on the lawn. And, yes, they are part of the kitchen."

"Should we go see what's going on?" Greg asked.

"I don't want to complicate things. You don't technically own the property yet, so let's wait and in the meantime, I'll call the agent."

No answer. My stress levels were rising, this was awkward AF.

Naked Joshua continued to exhibit no signs of calming down. His agitation was escalating with each passing moment. Tension lingered thick in the air.

"I wonder who called the cops," Greg mused.

I looked around. Across the street, set back on a neatly manicured lawn, was a ranch-style house. An older middle-aged woman in a flowered housedress stood on the front porch, hands on her hips. "Over there. I'll bet it was her."

Greg laughed. "I guess it's good to have nosey neighbors."

"Not really a good selling point," I joked, "but in this case, yes."

"I'm going to call the owner this time since the agent is not responding and let him know what's going on," I said to Greg. "I'm sure this isn't what he thinks is happening this morning."

When I explained the scene to the owner, he sighed. "Damn it, Joshua." I had a feeling this wasn't the first time Joshua had screwed up. "I'll be right over."

A few moments later, a silver BMW pulled up behind us at the curb. The owner, a graying, well-dressed man in his sixties, jumped out and headed toward Joshua and the police who were still interrogating him.

We couldn't catch a single word of their exchange, but after a few minutes, the owner strolled over to my car and waved like he was hailing a cab. I rolled down my window, wondering what he could possibly say.

"I'm so sorry about this," he said. "My son has some issues with substances. He thought when I said the house had to be empty by today that he was supposed to remove all of the cabinets and fixtures. For some reason, he thought he could get everything done this morning. Thank God he hadn't got to the toilets and sinks yet."

"Oh, yes, thank God for that," I agreed, trying not to roll my eyes. "This complicates the closing, though. And we still need to do the walk-through."

"Yes, of course."

Greg and I stepped out of the car. I noticed the neighbor across the street still standing on her porch. She had one hand over her mouth and the other on her hip. Her head was slowly shaking back and forth. If disapproval had an image, she was it.

When the owner noticed her and waved, she threw her hands up in the air and retreated into her house.

The officers had secured Joshua into the police car and motioned for the owner. We took the opportunity to start our walk-through. The front rooms were empty and clean, the primary suite likewise. The back bedroom and bathroom were Joshua's domain. In the bedroom, a pile of dirty clothes lay on the floor next to a bare, stained mattress. The bathroom could benefit from a thorough cleaning but was otherwise undamaged.

"It's the kitchen I really want to see," Greg said. I could feel his impatience. I hoped if he saw that most of the house was in good condition, the kitchen wouldn't cause him to back out of the purchase.

I followed Greg through the dining room to the kitchen holding my breath the whole way. The hung cabinets above the counters were missing, and the sink had been pulled from its base and sat on the island. The countertop had been lifted and sat at an angle above the floor cabinets. I waited for Greg's reaction.

"It could be worse," he said.

"I really should thank that neighbor for calling the police."

"So, what happens now?" Greg asked.

"We can either have the owner make the repairs and wait until they are done to close, or we can make a deal with the owner to reduce the price and you can have the work completed after we close."

"Option B sounds more doable. I need to get my stuff out of storage ASAP."

The owner walked into the kitchen. "I'm so sorry. I should not have trusted my son to follow through. This is a mess. I will get this cleaned up!"

Following our brief discussion, Greg and I made our way out the front door. The owner, visibly embarrassed yet relieved that the deal remained intact in spite of his son's recklessness.

"I'll coordinate with your agent to schedule a new closing date and arrange for a credit to cover the damages," I assured, feeling grateful that the sale was still on track and my client was happy.

The closing was only delayed by a couple of days, but Greg didn't mind after all. As we walked into the title company to sign documents, Greg whispered, "I was thinking of remodeling the entire kitchen anyway. Now I get my new cabinets all paid for."

MENTAL NOTE:
Say no to drugs.

8

Driving Miss Daisy

hirley was a client whose home I listed just before COVID hit. During one of my visits to the property to install the lockbox, I needed to grab the spare key from her. Before I even had the chance to knock, Shirley swung open the front door, beaming with a wide smile and arms outstretched for a hug. This woman exuded sweetness and an overwhelming friendliness. Once she got started on certain topics, you could forget about making it home in time for dinner. Shirley and her family were incredibly passionate about their beliefs and on this particular visit, it was time for their pitch.

Shirley and her adult children felt a profound responsibility to save me. Three of the kids still resided with her, while one had already moved out. However, all four were present for a family member's birthday celebration scheduled for later that evening. In this business, it's often beneficial to be adaptable and possess the ability to embody multiple personalities, much like a chameleon. A psychology degree would also be valuable in this field.

While I lean towards a more spiritual outlook, I listened attentively to their prayers, remaining open-minded. The moment was nice, yet my nerves were tingling as if I were about to step onto a public speaking stage.

Once saved, I was ready to take on the world! I tried to find a suitable smaller property for Shirley to purchase, but she saw nothing that interested her. In the meantime, I secured a six-month rental for her so we could continue looking. The family

dog made the rental difficult. What landlord wouldn't want an eighty-pound Pit bull in their rental home? Her children and even her ex-husband came together to assist with moving her belongings, showing a commendable sense of support and cooperation.

The sale of her home proceeded swiftly, without any major issues, until the day of closing when unforeseen complications arose.

Even though she had moved into a rental, the new homeowners found her sitting on the floor in their living room. "I don't want to sell. I'm not selling my house," she announced.

The buyers' agent let me know what was happening. Luckily, we had worked together before, so she was sympathetic to my situation, but at the same time advocating for her clients.

I arrived at the house and pleaded with Shirley to leave. "We have officially closed, Shirley. It's not your house anymore. You are trespassing."

She glared at me. "I thought you would be on my side. Some Christian you are."

I could see I wasn't getting anywhere with her. The new owners were pacing nervously in the kitchen. This moment was *way* more awkward than the naked guy on crack who wreaked havoc on my client's property. I felt bad for them and decided to call Shirley's ex-husband. According to her kids, even though they were divorced, he still held some sway with her.

Minutes later, he arrived. He took a deep breath as he walked into the room. I wasn't sure if that meant the situation would improve or get worse, but after a brief discussion, he was able to calm her down. "We've talked about this. Yvonne found

you a beautiful rental to live in while you look for a new home, something more manageable now that you are on your own."

"But I am happy here."

Her ex paused. "Maybe God wants you to find a new place and meet new people. Did you think of that?"

Shirley smiled and her eyebrows raised. I could sense her processing this information. She left shortly after that. I thanked Shirley's ex-husband for his help. The new owners ventured out of the kitchen expressing their gratitude to both of us amidst exchanged apologies. It was a moment of mutual understanding and goodwill as we acknowledged any unintended inconveniences or discomfort that had arisen during the process.

Unfortunately, that incident was only part one. As her buyer's agent, I had less than six months to match Shirley with a home. That would have been hard enough given her exacting desires, but COVID complicated things even more.

Following COVID protocols with masks and gloves, I showed Shirley many properties that fit her general wants, but none seemed to hit the spot. She wanted a single-level home on an acre lot just outside of town, secluded and with at least five bedrooms. At one of the open houses in BFE, we ran into another agent who smiled and said, "Hi, Shirley."

"You know each other?" I asked. They nodded.

When Shirley wandered off to look at another room, the agent pulled me aside. "I showed her forty properties a few years ago, and they never bought. If I were you, I'd run for the hills."

"I just sold her primary residence," I countered.

"I'm shocked. Maybe you can get her to buy this one."

However, that wasn't the case. Four months into her rental lease, we found ourselves visiting the twenty-third property that I thought might sufficiently meet her needs and preferences. Yes, twenty-three. At this point, everything began to blur together, and it felt like I had logged over 2,000 miles on my car in just one week. This meticulous search for the perfect home for a picky buyer was proving to be quite the journey. I had to consciously refrain from using swear words, vowing to keep my thoughts to myself.

Before entering the house, we put on our masks and gloves as usual, but for this property, we also were required to put on shoe covers due to the homeowner being in remission from cancer. The current owner, who still lived at the property, was purposely not at home out of an abundance of caution.

As we toured the cozy, well-kept property, Shirley asked, "Why is this one for sale? It's so nice!"

"According to the listing agent, the seller needs to move closer to family due to health reasons." I kept the cancer information to myself.

"Oh dear. Poor man. It is such a lovely home. Let me think about this for a couple of days. I will let you know. I'm thinking this is the one."

"Don't delay too long. Someone else could snap it up," I cautioned.

"If God intends for me to have it, it will be here."

With that, Shirley got into her car and drove off. I locked up, removed my mask and gloves, and left the property hopeful that Shirley would proceed with an offer.

Two days later, I got a call from the property's listing agent.

"Your client showed up at the house on Dixon and aggravated my seller."

"What? I had no idea she went over there! She knows she's not supposed to go to properties without me and unannounced."

"Apparently, she forced my client to take some religious pamphlets and tried to get him to accept Jesus so Jesus would cure him of his ailments. My client tried talking to her through the doorbell intercom, but the lady wouldn't leave until he opened the door and took her pamphlets. This went on for twenty minutes. My client is afraid she'll show up again."

"Good grief. I will call Shirley and let her know not to continue."

I called Shirley immediately and, in my calmest voice, tried to explain the rules of property viewing.

She claimed she wasn't there to view the property, just to visit the owner and share her good news religious pamphlets. "I was trying to help him," she argued.

"But you must have an appointment and be accompanied by me," I explained. "We need permission to visit the property."

Her voice got louder and more aggressive. "I don't need anyone's permission to visit someone," she snorted. "It's a free country. And how did you find out about my visit anyway?"

"The listing agent informed me," I replied, "after the homeowner called her."

"What's her name? I'm calling her right now," Shirley yelled into the phone.

I was obligated to share that information, which I did. But at that point, I knew I couldn't continue with Shirley as a client. I couldn't find the perfect house anyway.

I called the listing agent immediately and warned her about the call she was going to get. I found out later it was several calls over a few days, and Shirley did not put an offer on the house.

After the dust settled, I reached out to Shirley to let her know that I was not able to help her, that my attempts to find her a new home were unsuccessful.

No answer.

I left her the sweetest voicemail, the kind that when you hang up you wonder, "Who Am I?" because you're never that nice in real life. Despite not receiving a response, I take comfort in knowing that I gave it my best effort.

MENTAL NOTE:
You are not required to set yourself on fire to keep others warm.

9

Code of Ethics

Sometimes, a real estate agent-client relationship lasts a long time and involves many purchases. I worked with Jim for about five years, finding him several properties to invest in. He owned a construction company that specialized in rehabbing distressed properties and always did a first-class job. Whenever a distressed property showed up on or off the market, he wanted to be notified asap.

The last time, I found him an excellent flip opportunity. The modest single-family home had been through a flood and was already partially remediated.

"What do you think?" I asked Jim after finishing the tour.

"It has potential," he replied. I watched as his eyes surveyed the outside of the house. He had the serious face of a man calculating expenses versus profit in his head. "Let's make an offer. Lower than the asking. We'll see what they counter."

"Great. I'll get right on it."

A week went by with no communication from the seller's agent, which was very unusual. I attempted to reach out to her broker but received no response. Resorting to social media, I discovered that her absence was due to the recent birth of her child. Despite this, we submitted a new offer, as our previous one had expired. Regrettably, the offer was promptly declined, at least I knew the seller was alive. I reached out to Jim to inform him that our second offer had been turned down.

"What was their counteroffer?" Jim asked.

"There wasn't one."

"What? Do they even want to sell it?" Jim sounded incredulous. "Forget it."

Our offer wasn't unreasonably low, but it seemed like the seller was firm on their asking price, even though the property had been on the market for months. I did not know the seller's agent personally, not sure why they did not counter us. I knew Jim was interested in the property; but he wasn't into playing games. I had to agree. It wouldn't bother Jim if he didn't get it. He had several crews working on properties at any given time.

Three months later, I noticed the property was still for sale for the same price. It's unusual for a property to be on the market for that long without a price reduction.

I thought I should let Jim know, but I got busy with other clients and put off calling him till after the weekend. When I looked up the listing again before calling Jim, the price had been slightly reduced.

"Should we put in an offer," I asked him.

"Yes. Make it the same as our first offer and let's see what happens."

I had to laugh at his mischievous attitude. Now he was willing to play, at least a little.

With the offer submitted, I waited for a response. I hoped for a response. Third time's a charm, right?

I didn't have to wait long.

"Yvonne, this is Linda. I'm reaching out to you as a professional courtesy."

My mind was racing, trying to guess what she was about to say so I could have a response ready.

She continued. "We received your offer on the Hastings

property. That's all good. What I felt you should know is that your client called me the day before your offer showed up and wanted me to represent him hoping to get a better deal."

"Oh really? What did you tell him?"

"I said no I wouldn't represent him because he was already working with you. I said I would only accept an offer from another agent if I had a signed Release of Agency Representation from you. And then, can you believe this, he reached out to my seller directly! Tried to cut us both out of the deal."

I bit my tongue to keep my thoughts internal. After a deep breath, I responded, "Is no one loyal anymore?"

"Money speaks louder sometimes," Linda said. "Especially in this business."

"So true. Thank you for letting me know, Linda."

"I know how hard we work to make a sale. It burns me when buyers and sellers think we do this for free."

"I hear you. So is your client going to entertain our third offer?"

"I will present it and get back to you."

"Thank you, appreciate your efforts."

As I contemplated confronting Jim about his cunning tactics, various approaches came to mind.. Yet, I understood the allure of saving money; it's a common desire. Ultimately, I chose to let it go and act as if nothing happened.

To my surprise, our third offer was met with a counter, and Jim promptly agreed to it! It was a cash deal with a fast closing, marking the end of our six-month journey with this house. Now, all that remained was for Jim to finish the remodel, and for me to list the property for sale. Here's hoping.

Just a short month later, my phone rang, and it was Jim on the line.

"Yvonne, I appreciate you helping me with the Hastings property, but I'm going to try selling it myself first. Give me three months and if I can't sell it, I'd like to have you list it."

"Sounds good." I was ok with this plan because the price he wanted was way over market value and I probably wouldn't be able to sell it.

Unfortunately for Jim, the property failed to sell. Instead of genuine buyers, he found himself inundated with inquiries from agents looking to list it for him. Frustrated with the process, he eventually realized it was time to reach out to me for assistance.

After I listed the remodeled home, we quickly attracted interest, and within a few weeks, we had a contract with a wonderful family. It goes to show that pricing is key, and I'm thrilled that everything ultimately fell into place.

MENTAL NOTE:
Loyalty is rare . . . everyone wants a deal!

10

Double-edged Sword

The phone started ringing, and although I didn't recognize the number, I picked it up without hesitation. You never know when it might turn into a potential sale.

"Hello, this is Yvonne," I answered in my business casual voice.

The heavily accented voice on the other end tried to get me to buy a list of verified buyers and sellers. How this spam got through the filter, I'll never know, but this happens at least twice a day.

"No thank you," I said before hanging up, not giving the caller a chance to continue with "a better offer." I told myself I will start letting phone calls go to voicemail even when I'm sitting at my desk, but I can't. I'm just not programmed that way. Most of the time, I enjoy interacting with people. Just not telemarketers who barely speak English.

My *Spam Likely* alert usually catches these calls, but occasionally one gets through. I try to be polite. It is someone trying to earn a living, but I don't have time to waste when I know I don't want what they are selling.

Another go-to way to get off the call is to pretend I have bad reception and keep repeating, "Hello?"

I scan the list of incoming emails. So many offers to buy magazine advertising. *Only $1,950 a page,* this one says, *to be a featured agent.* What they don't say is that they'll feature fifty other agents in the same issue. They try to butter me up saying I've been chosen for this offer because of my top agent status.

The funny thing is, they never say how they arrived at the top agent listings or how many agents received the same "honor" that month.

Another call came in. A mortgage broker's "assistant" was calling to schedule a coffee date with the lender. I recognized the number. It's a service from Taiwan.

"If Mr. Phelps wants a coffee date, have him call me directly," I said. I can pretty much guarantee this will not happen.

The most interesting encounters are those internet leads arriving via email, often from people interested in having their vacant land listed. It's astonishing how scammers will go to great lengths, even sending fake driver's licenses or passports. Can you imagine if your land was being sold without your knowledge? To ensure authenticity, I always try to engage in a phone call with them (which typically scares them off) and insist on verifying their identity with two forms of ID before proceeding.

Other calls and excessive amounts of texts I receive are from brokerages (who will remain nameless, but one starts with an E) trying to recruit me to join their team. They offer countless leads, claim they are the best in town, etc. Oh, and I can't forget the random investors blowing me up looking to buy distressed single-family homes with cash. Make it stop!

This is worse than listening to the radio. Commercials are a trigger for me. Apologies for this venting session. Ha-ha, I'm sure many can relate.

To be fair, I do send out advertising myself. I try to be unobtrusive to a degree. If I have a new listing or have just sold in an area, I will send out postcards. People do get upset about this. They could just throw the postcard away, but they create such drama.

"How did you get my address?"

"I'll report you to your broker and association. You'll lose your license."

I wonder what causes some people to react like that over one piece of mail. OK, so my postcard was the twentieth one they received that week. Maybe I'm just the lucky agent to be their last straw. I guess, mathematically, I shouldn't get too upset. If I sent a hundred postcards and got one complaint, that's only one percent negative. I feel better when there is at least one positive lead from the cards, but that doesn't always happen.

MENTAL NOTE:
Time is a finite commodity. Manage it well.

11

Grandma's House

I firmly believe in the saying "Your network is your net worth."

Although our local women's networking events might not always result in immediate real estate transactions, they serve as valuable platforms for promoting my services. Frequently, I've been able to capitalize on potential leads that arise. Additionally, these gatherings help me connect with fellow female entrepreneurs in the community, fostering mutual support and contributing to the growth of our local business network.

At our event last May, I sat at a table with several impressive women. We introduced ourselves to the new attendees. One of those attendees was Bethany, a bridal boutique owner. Her shop had built a solid reputation in the area.

Upon my introduction and discussion of my real estate business, she revealed that her grandmother, aged ninety-two, had recently passed away, leaving her the inheritance of her grandmother's house.

"I would love for you to help me sell it," Bethany said with a questioning tone.

When she told me where it was, on the west side about an hour outside my usual sales territory, I agreed to take a look at it. The west side had a known reputation for being less safe. Drive-by shootings were frequent, and the area was decorated with lots of colorful graffiti. However, there was a possibility that one of my investors could acquire it before I even listed it on the MLS.

Bethany and I met that Wednesday morning at the property. Describing it as run-down would be generous. It looked to be one of the oldest houses in the area, pre-building boom. It was a two-story farmhouse style (without the farm). The front porch roof drooped in multiple places, and the paint was peeling so much that the previous beige was threatening to take over the light blue. Shrubs were overgrown and the front walk was barely visible under a layer of dead grass and weeds.

"It's in rather rough condition," Bethany apologized. "Grandma grew up poor and liked to hold on to things. She never liked to spend money unless it was absolutely necessary. We used to joke about her collections being absolutely necessary. But I know those things brought her joy, so we let it go."

I could see Bethany's eyes getting glassy as she spoke.

"Were you close?" I asked.

"I'm her only granddaughter, so yeah, my mother used to call us two peas in a pod. Grandma always told me not to wait to get married to own a home, but I never seemed to get out of the renting habit. I think this was Grandma's way of getting me into my own home. Unfortunately, it's not where I want to live, even if I did fix it up. She'd be sad to know that, but at least if I sell it, I'll have money for my own place."

I tried to lighten the mood. "That's so true. And sometimes these sell quickly," I assured her. "House flippers are always looking for deals. I get numerous calls every week from investors asking if I have anything distressed or off-market."

We walked through the house. Every room was filled with her grandmother's belongings, threadbare chairs, overfilled China cabinets, stacks of books and papers, hundreds of framed photos, and shelves filled with knick-knacks. The closets, filled to the brim with clothes and shoes, emitted a distinctive odor of mothballs, reminiscent of having Grandma standing right beside me, watching my every move. "Would you like some Werther's Originals, dear?" I could imagine her saying to me and I felt her presence in the house. While the term "hoarder" crossed my mind, I refrained from uttering it, not wishing to cause offense.

"My grandmother was certainly a collector," Bethany offered, pointing to a glass-paned China cabinet packed with dozens of troll dolls standing shoulder to shoulder. "I don't really know where to begin."

"First, go through the house and remove everything you want to keep," I explained. "Then the rest can be donated or sold at an estate sale. I can help you set that up."

"That would be great. My husband thinks I inherited a problem more than a gift."

"In a way, he is right, but problems have solutions, and we'll get this problem solved. It may take a little while. I might actually know someone who would be interested in this property. He likes properties like this."

I gave my client, Martin, a call and he drove out to the house to look it over.

"It has possibilities," he said. "Let's get an inspector over here and we'll go from there."

Bethany was delighted. Over the next couple of weeks Bethany and I, and occasionally her two teen sons cleaned and organized the house contents as much as possible. They brought dozens of boxes which we filled and labeled. I coordinated

Goodwill drop-offs and the estate sale setup. Once we cleared the piles of clutter from around and on top of the baby grand piano, I made a few calls and found a buyer for it. They got a good deal, but we were glad it was gone.

In the laundry room, I noticed some water damage to the floor tiles. "We should probably get that checked out." The floor had a little give and a squeak. I hoped it was sturdy enough to be walking on. We weren't as light as Bethany's frail grandmother had been.

Bethany sighed. "Grandma never mentioned a leak."

The boys spent one evening pulling cacti that had taken root throughout the neglected lawn. At one time, the lawn had turf, now a dried carpet, and frankly, a fire hazard. The boys also gave a serious trim to the overgrown Brittlebush and Texas Sage surrounding the house.

Chris, Bethany's husband, barely spoke to me when the both of us were at the house. He would send Bethany to ask me questions. *I'm not that scary!* Ever met someone and struggled to gauge their personality? It's like they're super introverted, avoiding eye contact, leaving you wondering, *Am I Medusa? Will you turn to stone if you look at me?*

On one occasion, I overheard him ask Bethany, "Are you sure she knows what she's doing?" *Not scary, I guess. He thinks I'm incompetent.*

The estate sale was set up and advertised for one long weekend, from Friday to Sunday. The weather was sunny and fair which helped make for a great turnout and many sales. At the end of the weekend, a local auction house offered a price for all remaining contents and took it away in two large trucks.

Martin, my buyer, ended up making an offer and hired a home inspection service. Bethany and I did a last sweep and mop before they arrived.

Three days later, I received an email from Martin. He's backing out of the deal. The home inspection found serious mold in the primary bathroom, kitchen, and laundry area. It had permeated the walls behind cabinets and into the pantry area. Apparently, an unrepaired leak allowed water to seep in over a long time. The mold was pervasive. Martin wrote that the cost of removing the mold would make flipping the house a losing proposition.

When I notified Bethany, I could tell from her voice that her heart sank.

"I might have another possible buyer, though. One with mold experience. You must disclose this to potential buyers.," I explained. "The mold should be removed before going on the market."

I took the second possible buyer out to the property, but he passed on it as well. I let Bethany know it was a no-go. "I can recommend a mold remediation service."

"Yes, please."

"I'll send you the info. Once that's taken care of, we can put the house on the market and you're sure to get a better price for it."

"I hope so after all of this," Bethany replied.

* * *

Weeks went by with no word. Weeks became months. I didn't want to press the issue. The family was grieving their loss.

Then out of the blue, I got a call from Bethany.

We exchanged pleasantries, then she dropped the bombshell. "My husband has decided he'd rather work with a male real estate agent." I thought, *Fine by me. Selling black mold isn't my forte.*

I considered having a conversation with her husband about the weeks I spent assisting with cleaning and organizing donations for the estate sale, all without any compensation, based on our verbal agreement that I would be the listing agent. However, I refrained from doing so. I sensed that he wouldn't be interested in my perspective. *I'm just a woman.*

Well, on the other hand I've fulfilled my good deeds for the month by providing community service for Bethany and her family. Lesson learned: always get things in writing. It's interesting that Bethany's husband was the one to relay the update through her. Equally interesting is Bethany's absence from the networking events. Haven't seen her since.

MENTAL NOTE:
Consult all parties involved before making moves.

12

The Unlikely Debt

Open houses are a great way to meet potential clients. I met Jeri at one of my properties listed for sale. She admitted that she was looking at random listings, not even sure exactly what she was searching for. When she saw an open house, she checked it out. "Less pressure," she admitted.

I could see she wasn't in a hurry, so I tried to pull a few hints from her as we toured the house.

"I'll know it when I see it," she said.

Not helpful, I thought. She was friendly, and after a while, I did get a sense of her preferences. She was married with two girls ages four and six, a business professional, and an avid gardener.

"My husband is an artist," she offered. "His income is sporadic, and qualifying for a loan would be problematic. So, I'm buying the house in my name."

Smart. Her position as a retail buyer for a major chain meant she was in the habit of making important decisions.

She didn't have an agent and wasn't prequalified. I extended an offer to become her agent and connect her with three of my top mortgage brokers to initiate the lending process.

"It's beneficial to ensure loan qualification before embarking on property searches and making offers on homes," I elaborated. "Having that assurance greatly streamlines the process when you do come across something you love."

Jeri ultimately opted for my good friend Jeff as her lender. She noted his prompt response to her call, answering on the first ring, and how they quickly established a great connection. With the loan process officially underway, it was time to begin the shopping journey.

After showing Jeri a couple of properties that matched her preferences, she was able to refine her wish list. It worked in my favor that Jeri liked to talk. It made the viewing process enjoyable as well as informative.

A new listing appeared in the area where Jeri was looking. A short sale that was, in my opinion, priced to sell quickly. I set up an appointment to tour the property.

Jeri did a lot of smiling and nodding as we made our way through the rooms. The owners, though still living there, had minimal furnishings in the rooms and personal items were out of sight. It almost looked staged, though not likely for a short sale.

Overall, the property wasn't extravagant, but it was spacious and thoughtfully arranged. It had a Mid-Century Modern feel with a touch of Scandinavian design, reminiscent of an Ikea showroom. The backyard was expansive, about a half-acre, featuring a rectangular, in-ground pool and a sizable shed.

"That would make a great studio for Pete," Jeri said. Other than a few comments, there was a noticeable lack of conversation this time. My curiosity was piqued.

"Well, Jeri, you've not said much today. I did most of the talking."

"I think we could live here," she said. "I like the open floor plan so I can keep an eye on the girls. And the enclosed backyard where they can play and not wander off. What is the next step? How do we seal the deal, as they say?"

"First, I would need your prequalification to submit the offer. I don't think we should make too low an offer. It seems priced to sell already. Have you received your PQF from the lender yet?"

"Not yet. Will that mess things up?"

"Yes, without that form we can't submit. But don't worry. You have already submitted what the lender needs so he can prepare it in an hour or so. The sellers want this to close quickly, so that's in our favor."

That's when Jeri made a request. "My current lease is running out. Do you think the owner would let me move in before the closing?"

I suddenly realized I was holding my breath. I exhaled. "I will ask. Sometimes it's possible." Usually, I try to avoid pre-possessions, but Jeri gave no reason why there would be a problem.

The owners agreed to a prepossession without hesitation. They wanted to sell the place and get out from under the mortgage. They moved out and had the place empty and clean before Jeri's move-in date, a week before closing.

On the day before Jeri's pre-possession, I got a call from my lender friend, Jeff, who was Jeri's loan officer.

"Yvonne, we have a problem. Jeri's loan has a contingency."

"What? Why?"

"Well," he paused, "there's something she needs to take care of. I'm hoping she can take care of it. I'm working on it. Jeri is on her way over. We'll try to get it straightened out ASAP."

"I hope so, Jeff, or Jeri and her family will be on the street. Their lease expires tomorrow. All of their stuff is in a pod." I didn't say it out loud, but I could have yelled at myself for arranging a pre-possession. "Keep me posted," I added and hung up.

I knew Jeff was great at his job. If there is a way, he'll find it. He has never let me down. Yet.

I kept busy with other matters but with one ear paying attention to my phone. Hours went by. Nothing. I kept picturing Jeri, her husband, and her kids sleeping in her car in some parking lot. I hadn't met the girls, but I pictured two whiney uncomfortable preschoolers climbing all over their stressed parents. One night wouldn't be so bad, but if the loan doesn't go through, they are stuck. On my laptop, I pulled up area apartment listings just in case. There's bound to be a month-to-month available somewhere.

I was just about to stop for dinner when Jeri's number flashed on my phone.

"Good news, I hope?" I asked.

"It took a while, but yes, I got everything straightened out!"

"If you don't mind my asking, what was the issue?"

"The issue was a $4.11 utility bill that was sent to collection over six years ago."

"That was it?" I asked. "Wow! To think that would stop a house sale. I'm not sure where I first heard this saying or if I came up with it myself, but it's undeniably accurate: In real estate, it's all black and white; there's no room for gray areas."

"I certainly found that out," Jeri said with a laugh. She continued, "I went with Jeff, your loan officer friend, to APS and we negotiated, well, Jeff negotiated the bill and four hours later we were able to get clear to close."

"Four hours. Wow. But you'll have a house now."

"Yes, thankfully."

I envisioned Jeff in his sharp suit and polished Prada shoes, confidently engaging with the utility's office clerk. He consistently exuded a professional demeanor and carried himself with a no-nonsense attitude. It was clear not to provoke him, he had zero tolerance for absurd situations, a sentiment I could completely empathize with. I could imagine his face scrunching up as if his eyebrows were ready to attack while he attempted to reason with the clerk over a ridiculous bill from over 6 years ago.

After my conversation with Jeri, I called Jeff. "Jeff, you are a lifesaver. I owe you one." He knew exactly what I was talking about.

"That makes three you owe me," he teased. "Happy hour on Friday?"

"Sure."

MENTAL NOTE:
If there is a will, there is a way.

13

New License, No Problem

My client, Jack, was a newcomer to the buying and flipping scene, but he told me he had sufficient funds at his disposal. With a background in new home construction, he was well-equipped for the remodeling aspect of the project. However, lacking in design expertise, I offered my assistance. Drawing from my experience in design and having graduated from FIDM with a degree in design (though primarily a fashion school, I also pursued interior design courses), I was confident in providing valuable guidance.

I found a promising property with significant potential, and Jack decided to move forward with purchasing the home. We joined forces to tackle the demolition phase together. Jack was pleased with the vision of my designs, showing authentic excitement for the project.

"Your finishing touches are great," Jack said. "If it were up to me, it would be pretty boring."

"Don't sell yourself short," I replied. "You've worked on a lot of houses. I think you have a good sense of what works."

The house was only on the market for a few days before it was sold. With that success, Jack was eager to move ahead with another property.

Shortly after the initial sale, I found another property located down the street from the first one. Since Jack's funds were tied up in another construction project, he had to opt for a loan to purchase this property. His intention was to expand it with a 1500 square foot addition.

"If this place sells as quick as the last, it will be worth it," Jack said.

The property, being off market, had an unrepresented seller who was very cooperative, making the transaction easy. We swiftly closed the deal within 10 days, setting the project in motion. With a demo party to kick things off, work commenced promptly. Jack expressed confidence in his ability to handle the interior design himself and voiced his gratitude for my prior assistance.

"You know where I am if you need me," I told him.

"Will do."

I checked in on Jack after a few weeks.

"I've been having trouble with the permits being delayed. We haven't started on the addition yet, but we are making progress on the remodel," he explained.

"That happens sometimes, as you probably know from your construction jobs."

"Not usually my problem. That's for the big bosses."

I checked in with Jack every week or so. I wanted to keep our connection so I could list it as soon as possible.

"Yvonne," Jack asked on a call, "does this happen often? I'm stressing out. I had hoped to sell this place by now. That hard money loan is very high interest. It's killing me."

"I'll swing by this afternoon and see if I can offer any suggestions."

"Great."

When I arrived, Jack's crew was at work in the main house. The addition shell was complete and the wall studs were up, but no drywall.

"We're waiting for the electrical inspection. A week now," Jack said. I could hear the frustration in his tone.

A blond woman, a little older than me, walked into the addition.

"This is Greta, my girlfriend," Jack said.

"I've heard all about you," Greta said, extending her hand.

We shook, but at the same time I wondered what Jack could know *all* about me.

"Greta's getting her real estate license," Jack said, proudly. "Almost there."

"Jack says we'll make a great team. He fixes, and I sell."

"Sounds great." I forced out with the most insincere smile I could muster. Inside, I was furious, feeling like steam was about to erupt from the top of my head.

We toured the main house so I could see the progress so far. I swear, Jack is colorblind. The main room had a natural red brick accent wall, but Jack had used a patterned tile that clashed. Every room seemed to have a different set of clashing patterns.

"I picked everything out myself," Jack boasted.

"And you were worried you would be boring," I replied.

A couple of weeks later, Jack called me to let me know he wouldn't be needing my services as a listing agent. Greta got her license and would be listing it.

"I had a feeling that was the plan," I said.

"No hard feelings?" he asked.

"None," I said, "It sounds like you two have a good plan. I will be bringing potential buyers by when you have it on the market."

"Please do."

I felt let down, but let's be honest... I was absolutely infuriated! I had invested a significant amount of time, not to mention I was the one who discovered the property in the first place.

Greta repeatedly reached out to me for assistance with various forms, procedures, and MLS listing protocols, tasks she should have been familiar with by now. While I remained polite, I consistently redirected her to seek guidance from her broker.

After ten months, the house was finally ready to be listed. Jack extended an invitation for me to preview it. The clashing patterns, numerous mismatched items, and outdated nickel fixtures left me feeling dizzy. Regrettably, the addition did little to enhance the home; instead, it seemed to disrupt the flow of the floorplan, making it feel awkward and disjointed.

Jack, concerned about his mounting expenses, decided to list the property at a whopping $150,000 above its reasonable value. Despite my best efforts, I couldn't find a buyer for the house. Even after six months, it lingered on the market. What occurred afterward was a mystery to me.

One day, while having lunch with a colleague, I was taken aback to find Greta as our server. She informed me that she and Jack had split up, and her real estate aspirations hadn't panned out, leading her back to serving. As for the never-ending project, it eventually sold for half its value, and Jack abandoned his flip attempts.

MENTAL NOTE:
The universe has a way of balancing the scales.

14

Secret Admirer

'm cautious by nature, especially after living in Los Angeles for ten years. Yet, as a real estate broker, I encounter individuals with unique stories and backgrounds. While most interactions are pleasant and centered around property transactions, there's always a small fraction of eccentric individuals whose interests lie far from real estate.

When I was a new agent, still in the process of learning the ropes, I found myself in a lively real estate office surrounded by seasoned professionals. Eager to secure new clients, I diligently answered every call that came my way.

During one specific call, instead of a legitimate inquiry in response to my greeting, all I heard was heavy breathing. Deciding it was inappropriate, I promptly hung up. Naturally, I shared the bizarre encounter with the other agents in the office.

"Goes with the territory," one said.

"Ignore it," said another.

"How would he even know me?" I asked.

"Perhaps, he stumbled upon your picture on Realtor.com or something and took a liking to what he saw."

"I didn't know Realtor.com was a dating site," someone joked.

"Maybe, I should not put up a headshot," I mused. In light of my marketing pictures, where I'm dressed professionally in a blazer and white collared shirt, it's amusing to think that perhaps it's just my face that's asking for it.

Over the next few weeks, the calls increased in frequency, the same heavy breathing, but from a different number each time. Sandy, another novice agent, explained that the caller was likely using a VoIP, A Voice Over Internet Protocol, number.

It wasn't just creepy; it was also frustrating. Unable to ignore my phone, I just wished for the unwanted calls to come to an end.

"Is there a way to trace the call to see where it is coming from?" I asked Sandy.

"Glen has a 'white pages' app that can track a call."

We enlisted Glen's help. It turned out the calls were local, coming from an address about two miles from where I live. The creep factor just went up a notch.

If I had someone else answer my phone, he just hung up. But I couldn't bother other agents every time my phone rang. Everyone has their own work to do.

The calls were often enough that I developed a routine. Hear a breath, hang up. Get on with my day. Until he spoke, sounding very angry.

"Yvonne... I would like to F&%$ you and &%$."

I hung up. The phone rang again. The same number. I hesitated, then answered.

"You like yoga. I see you." His deep voice was calm and measured now.

I hung up and blocked the number. Things were escalating. When he mentioned yoga, I figured he must have seen my Facebook page. That was better than my other thought, that he had followed me to my yoga class.

A few days later, I was at home minding my business when a FaceTime call came in. I didn't recognize the number. I set the phone on the table so the caller would only have a view of my white ceiling, but I could see the caller at an angle.

On camera was a man's hairy torso as he sat pleasuring himself while mumbling my name. I ended the call, blocked the number, and called the police.

I described the FaceTime call and gave the officer all of the information I had on the caller, the man's IP address, and all the days he had called my phone. I was informed by the officer that unless the man actually did something to harm me, there was little they could do. *Not helpful. What happened to protect and serve?*

One week later, as I was getting in my car at my house, I noticed a black garbage bag sitting next to the rear tire with a small teddy bear propped on top of it. The bear held a folded paper between its paws. My curiosity got the better of me. I unfolded the paper. In childlike writing, it read: *Yavonne, put this lingerie on and take photos and send it to this number. Your secret admirer.*

I was too creeped out to look in the bag. Thinking the police would act on this harassment, I took photos of the bear, the bag, and the note before I kicked it to the side of the driveway to deal with it later.

I reminded the officer on the phone who I was and that I had called about the phone pervert before. I described the bag and note.

"Now he knows where I live," I practically shouted into the phone. "He could come back."

"Ma'am," the officer said, "I could send a car to have a look, but there hasn't been a crime. There is little we can do."

"He's harassing me," I protested.

"And he will tell us that he's an admirer just trying to get your attention."

"And when I'm assaulted, raped, or killed, then you'll do something?"

"Ma'am, it's not likely to come to that," the officer said in a condescending tone.

"Not likely is not reassuring." I could feel myself getting more worked up the longer I talked to this guy. "Well, If you're sending that car, the bag is by the driveway. I'm getting out of here." I hung up.

I was living in a rental at the time. Luckily, my landlord was understanding and let me break my lease. She seemed more concerned about my safety than the police. I promised to recommend her to potential tenants.

Once I was able to screen calls, the caller eventually got bored and stopped calling. I never heard from him after that. Finally, after a year of harassment, I could relax when my phone rang. Unfortunately, that FaceTime image is still burned in my memory.

MENTAL NOTE:
Safety First! Screen unknown callers and always prioritize your safety by being vigilant about your surroundings.

15

Final Walkthrough

O ccasionally, individual buyers and sellers may negotiate terms outside conventional norms, particularly when mutual advantages are apparent. However, dealings with some major corporate buyers follow a different protocol. In my role as an agent representing the buyer aka "Closed Door Enterprises", a substantial real estate investment entity, I am well aware of their strict adherence to standard procedures. In this case, the buyer, Juan, was acquiring a property that I found in an off-market hoarding situation. Closed Door Enterprises' intention was to renovate and resell the property. Contracts were finalized, and the closing date was set.

The listing agent, who happened to be a friend of the seller, provided us with reassurance that the house would be thoroughly cleaned and vacant by the closing day, granting them a ten-day period to vacate. I came across this deal through the listing agent whom I met at a networking event. Although I hadn't previously engaged in any deals with her, she appeared competent, and the property itself proved to be a remarkable find, minus the owner's stuff everywhere.

On the morning of the closing day, I intended to do the final walkthrough at the hoarder's house. Given my buyer's unavailability, I proceeded alone, planning to utilize FaceTime to keep him informed throughout the inspection. Upon arrival, I was greeted by absolute chaos: belongings scattered everywhere with no sign of a moving truck. The driveway still housed a rusted-out car on blocks, while bikes and assorted toys littered the front lawn. The garage door stood open, revealing a cluttered interior stacked with unidentifiable piles and random furniture. Even by the neighborhood's standards, the scene was disorderly.

A woman wearing a pink ankle-length bathrobe, with smudged makeup and a cigarette in hand, stood on the sidewalk, visibly upset. Parking my car at the curb, I stepped out and made my way towards her. As I began walking up, the woman called out to me.

"Hey, are you here for the house?" The woman approached.

"My name is Yvonne, the buyer's agent. You're Daisy, right? We met a few weeks ago. I'm here to do the final walk through. It doesn't look like you are ready. The closing is today."

"My friend who is selling the house for me said she'd take care of everything, but I haven't heard from her. She doesn't answer my calls. I think she's just waiting to close to collect her money. I don't know what to do." More tears. I could see she was beyond stressed. Then she turned on me. "You're making a pretty penny off this sale. You should do something for your money."

"In my defense, we are technically on the same side. We both want this sale to happen. Right?"

She nodded. "Sorry."

This is one of those situations where my heart goes out to the seller, but at the same time, this problem needs to be dealt with and quickly. "Do you have a moving truck coming?" I asked.

"I thought my friend was taking care of that. She's the real estate expert. So much for her promises. I was wrong to trust a — well, I was wrong to trust her, I guess."

The annoyance in her tone was deep. I wanted to explain that arranging to move is not part of our job, but I didn't know their relationship well enough to comment. Instead, I suggested, "Let's take a walk through the house, then we'll come up with a plan."

I should have been prepared for the interior based on the condition of the lawn, but it was worse than I would have imagined. Rooms piled with disorganized heaps. I could see and smell dog feces among the scattered clothes, toys, and whatnot on the bedroom floors. Several dogs, Miniature Pinschers and Chihuahuas, followed me at a distance, barking their cute little protective barks.

"I wish I still had foster kids to help me," Daisy said.

I was taken aback to think children lived here. My heart went out to them having to endure in such conditions. Also knowing this was better than the conditions they were coming from.

The kitchen needed a thorough scrubbing I was sure, but the counters were piled high with dishes, papers, food containers, and assorted random items. The ceiling near the stove was browned with grease stains, and the linoleum-tiled floor was heavily pockmarked.

I didn't want to add to the seller's stress, but I wondered if she knew the contract called for a $300 fee for each bag of garbage left behind after closing. And from the looks of it, all of her belongings would be considered garbage. By my estimate, there were about eighty bags worth. And the alternative, not closing on time, would result in huge penalties.

The backyard was in a similar state. A young man was collecting toys from the lawn and placing them in a large box.

"That's my nephew. He's the only one available to help."

"Good for him," I said. "I'll be right back. Keep packing."

I hopped into my car and called the seller's agent.

"We've got a huge problem. Your seller has been waiting for you to help her move. She has hardly started. You'd better get over here and get her moved out. You know the fees and penalties if she's not.

She promised to get on it. I assumed that the fear of her friend facing penalties, coupled with the despair she was experiencing, would motivate her. I found the nearest store and purchased boxes, tape, numerous garbage bags, and heavy-duty work gloves.

About a half hour after I returned to the property and got to work bagging up clothes with Daisy, her agent pulled up with a U-Haul, followed by a pickup with three people inside.

"Sorry about the mix-up, Daisy," she said. "Where should we start?"

I directed pairs to different locations, "Everything in bags and boxes out to the truck. Don't worry about sorting or neatness. We've got to move," I said. "Daisy can deal with all of it later."

We hustled until lunch. I sent Daisy's nephew to get pizzas (and more trash bags) while we worked. After a short break, we were back at it.

There was a knock on the door mid-afternoon. Daisy looked puzzled, so I went with her to answer it. She looked out the window. "It's Jim, my neighbor."

"Hi, Jim," Daisy said, opening the door. "What can I do for you?"

"What are you doing with that old Ford in the driveway?"

"I was hoping to sell it since my husband passed. Why?"

"I'd be willing to take it off your hands."

"For how much?"

Jim paused. I spoke up. "Daisy, at this point you'd be wise to just give it to him. If it's not gone by five o'clock, you'll be paying someone a lot to move it." I turned to Jim. "Can you move it right now?"

"As soon as I get my truck from the shop," he replied.

"Fine," said Daisy.

"Great," I said, putting a positive spin on it. "One less thing to worry about." What are the odds of a person showing up unannounced that solves a huge problem? It was an unbelievable stroke of luck.

After six hours and a U-Haul packed with boxes and trash bags, Daisy was finally on her way out. I considered my community service for the day complete. I photographed the empty place, FaceTime'd my client and got confirmation to go ahead and accept the premises. *Whew!*

MENTAL NOTE:
Teamwork makes the dream work.

16

Rats and Roaches, Oh My!

Most people like a challenge, but for my client Keith, the greater the challenge, the more he thrived. He had a love for tackling immense projects, particularly in his niche of purchasing and renovating dilapidated multi-family buildings. The more neglected the property, the more it appealed to him.

Browsing through online listings, I came across a fourplex located in a gritty section of downtown yet situated within a promising up-and-coming neighborhood. While three of the units were already occupied, the fourth end unit remained vacant. Though not having laid eyes on the property, my client was familiar with the area and was adamant about submitting an offer without hesitation.

"Let's do it," he urged. "I'm in."

The listing agent divulged that the property had lingered on the market for over 100 days primarily due to the existing leases, dissuading potential buyers. However, by the time Keith expressed interest, the leases had transitioned into month-to-month agreements. Should he opt to proceed, issuing a 30-day notice to vacate would suffice. Keith was unfazed by this issue, so I sent in his offer. The seller responded promptly, accepting all terms without delay.

Upon arrival at the property for inspection, we found that the images online painted a more favorable picture compared to the reality before us. As I gazed upon the property, I couldn't help but think, *This sure isn't 'Selling Sunset'*. The exterior was weathered, with peeling pale-yellow paint revealing gray cinder blocks beneath. The lawn was mostly dirt with patches of struggling grass attempting to grow. Surrounding the yards were chain-link fences and cracked sidewalks. The only cheerful sight was a multi-colored chalk hopscotch board drawn by kids on the concrete of unit number two.

"Let's start with the end unit," I suggested. "It's the empty one."

It was trashed. The condition of the unit was appalling. Spray paint symbols decorated the walls, while garbage littered the soiled floor. A sizable dark stain on the carpet in the middle of the living room hinted at an unconventional use, perhaps as an impromptu car repair space. It was evident that squatters had lived here at some point. I found myself holding my breath to avoid the odors and only daring to inhale when I was near a broken window. Despite the alarming situation, Keith remained calm.

"This has potential," he repeated several times as we walked through the rooms.

As we exited the unit, we were met by a woman standing in front of the next unit, glaring at us. She held a Pitbull that strained at the end of a thick chain leash. It growled and maintained a fierce gaze while it panted and bared its sharp white teeth.

The woman wore light blue sweatpants, visibly worn with several pulls and stains, paired with an ill-fitting, stained white top. Her greasy and matted hair completed the unkempt appearance.

"Get off my property," she barked. "I don't like strangers here." The Pitbull, with its bulging muscles, tugged on its leash, hoping to get in a bite, I was pretty sure.

"We're here to inspect. Your landlord said he notified you," I said.

"The landlord is a slumlord. Look at this place. Rats everywhere. The water doesn't work. Homeless crash in that last unit. Nasty people, addicts, thieves. The landlord does nothing except collect the rent. This is the last place you'd ever want to buy."

"That may be true, but we'd like to walk through your unit now," Keith said.

"You ain't coming inside, no way."

"Legally, we have the right to," Keith noted.

"Whoop tee doo," she said, laughing and throwing her arms in the air.

"Your name is Gloria, correct?" Keith asked. She stared at him when he used her name. "If there are rats, I'd like to see evidence. If the water doesn't work, I need to see about fixing it."

I could see her thinking about this. I bet she has been in this situation before where the landlord sells the building, and the tenants are forced to move out. She was not going to make this easy. She stepped in front of her door, pulling her dog with her.

Keith tapped me on the elbow and motioned to head to another apartment. Once we were out of earshot, he said, "There's other ways to deal with her."

The next unit's residents were the exact opposite of Pitbull lady. We introduced ourselves and were ushered inside. There were several children, all very young, and at least four adults living in this unit. They sat quietly and smiled at us as we passed by the rooms. Mattresses were on the floors in both bedrooms as well as the main living area and kitchen. Despite the number of people living here, the apartment was clean and tidy. They didn't have much in the way of material things, but they seemed to be a happy family.

"How is your water?" Keith asked the young woman giving us the tour. "Does it work?"

"Yes, but not always hot."

"Any pest problems?"

"The lady in three complains about rats and roaches, but I haven't seen any."

The apartment showed signs of extensive wear and tear, clearly in need of updating and repair. We observed missing doors, a cracked kitchen counter, broken windows, vertical blinds with missing blades, and even a missing shower head. It struck me that none of these issues had likely been reported to the landlord, possibly due to fear of rent increases to cover repair expenses.

I couldn't help but feel sympathy for the family facing displacement once Keith purchased the building. However, I reassured myself that there were other available housing options within their budget, likely in better condition.

"That unit wasn't in too bad a condition," Keith commented as we walked to Unit one. No one was home, so we let ourselves in. A quick walkthrough gave Keith the information he needed. There were shrines set up on tables with religious icons and pictures of saints arranged around candles. Keith lifted the throw rugs to discover the laminate flooring was very stained and scraped.

"This will all need to be replaced," he said. "I can get a deal on real wood. It'll be a nice upgrade. The non-load-bearing wall can be removed and open up this space."

When we stepped outside, we were greeted by the Pitbull lady and her dog again. This woman's intense energy, filled with anger and hostility, sent chills down my spine, leaving me thoroughly unsettled. She continued to badmouth the current landlord, ranting and screaming about the sorry state of the building for several minutes. Keith was having none of it.

"Ma'am, this is exactly the kind of property I like. I will be buying the building and I will be your new landlord."

She glared at him, muttered under her breath, and pulled her dog back to her apartment, slamming the door behind her.

We moved forward with the closing and gave each tenant a notice to vacate, Keith wanted to get started on renovations right away.

Gloria and her pitbull were not leaving even though she had not paid rent in four months, but with the help of the constable, we were able to evict her. Upon entering the apartment, it became apparent why she had resisted anyone going inside. The place was in shambles - walls and doors had been punched in, drug paraphernalia and used needles littered the floor and were embedded in the filthy carpet. Shockingly, there were even areas with human feces scattered around. Oh, and did I forget to mention the gruesome sight of a dead rat lying on the kitchen counter, impaled by a knife? I couldn't help but wonder whether this was her usual living standard or if the conditions happened due to the impending eviction. It felt like conditions similar to those in a third-world country, right in our own backyard. However, what saddened me the most was the dog having to endure such appalling conditions. It was a profoundly disheartening sight.

Once all the tenants had vacated, Keith's team swiftly renovated the property, and within a month, we had it fully rented out. Instead of being an eyesore in the neighborhood, the fourplex now stood as a shining example of what's achievable with the right investor and investment. Our success sparked a trend, inspiring other property owners in the area to follow suit and update their units as well.

MENTAL NOTE:
Don't believe everything you hear.

17

Bonnie and Clyde

Ron and Vera, a quirky duo, were referred to me by a commercial lender partner. For an older couple, they radiated an unconventional charm and were exceptionally talkative over the phone. They seemed excited to be seeking a luxury residence.

"Show us the best. I doubt anything on the market is beyond our budget," Ron said, laughing. He told me how he had made his millions. He was in the wholesale business and took a chance after hearing about a new virus becoming a problem. He invested hundreds of thousands in surgical and N-95 masks and gloves before COVID hit with a vengeance.

"You are a lucky man," I said.

"My wife and I have worked hard for many years, and it's finally paid off. Somebody is watching over us, for sure."

Claiming a net worth of fifty million, Ron provided me with his banker's contact details, crucial for verifying his funds, along with a screenshot of his bank account. His presentation appeared genuine, and I found myself placing greater trust in him, considering the reputable source of the referral.

The couple selected a few high-end homes in the area, and I scheduled a showing for their preferred option—a lakeside property—for the following day. While it was approximately 7000 square feet, notably smaller than the 10,000 they initially expressed a preference for, they seemed impressed by what they had seen online. Meanwhile, I reached out to Ron's banker, and to my relief, everything aligned with Ron's claims. His wealth was indeed as substantial as he had stated, with the banker promptly providing a proof of funds letter.

The following afternoon, I met Ron and Vera for the first time at the lakeside home, listed for ten million. They pulled into the circular drive in a weathered, silver Mercedes. While I found it peculiar, I brushed it off, acknowledging that some individuals develop strong attachments to their vehicles.

The property had been listed for a few months, with the owner/agent hosting open houses every weekend. During our visit, the owner was absent, but their assistant checked us in. As the owner resided in the house, all of their personal belongings were on display. In such instances, buyers were typically closely accompanied by the listing agents to navigate the tour.

We explored both the interior and exterior of the property. Ron's slight limp made our tour a leisurely one, but I didn't mind at all. They appeared intrigued by the place. The grand entryway, featuring a cathedral ceiling and elegant dropped lighting, offered a captivating introduction to the rest of the house. The open layout of the first floor created an illusion of spaciousness, while the floor-to-ceiling windows along the lake-facing wall enhanced the overall sense of openness. The breathtaking view of the lake against the backdrop of majestic mountains was truly awe-inspiring and seemed to justify the property's price tag.

"I love this place," Vera exclaimed.

At one point, when I was turned away referring to the listing brochure and pointing out the amenities, I caught them taking photos of each other posed near the soaring fieldstone fireplace.

I thought to myself, it's not really appropriate to be taking photos like that in front of the owner's agent/assistant.

"I just love this place," Vera repeated.

The second floor had four large bedrooms, each with its own ensuite. The lower level, open to the stone patio at the back of the house through sliding French doors, had a game room, a home theater, and a full bathroom, as well as an area that could be used for a home gym or whatever. The pool and backyard were magnificent. A stepped stone walkway descended gracefully to a wooden dock below. Tethered to the dock was a quaint pontoon boat, adding a charming touch to the serene scene.

"I love this place," Vera exclaimed again as she had several times during the tour. By the end of the tour, she was saying, "I have to have this place."

Ron nodded in agreement. "Let's put an offer on it then. Yvonne, how soon can we get the ball rolling?"

"On it right away," I assured him.

After departing from the open house, I returned to the office to finalize their paperwork. However, a nagging feeling in my gut prompted me to conduct some additional investigation before proceeding with their offer.

I reached out to my commercial lender to verify how she had come into contact with Ron and Vera. To my surprise, she mentioned they were referred by another lender whom she didn't have a close acquaintance with. Initially, I had assumed she knew these clients directly.

Concerned by the lack of response, I attempted to reach both the banker and Ron to confirm the banking information. However, neither of them answered my calls, nor did they return my messages.

When I contacted the owner of the property, I informed him that there was a couple interested in making an offer. However, I mentioned that I wanted to double check their proof of funds before proceeding further.

When I said the names Ron and Vera, he gasped. "My assistant mentioned they had come back to the open house. They've been here three or four times in the past month."

Now I was very suspicious. These individuals gave the impression that it was their first visit to the property, which left me feeling uncertain about their intentions.

I decided to conduct a Google search on Ron's bank. Being an out of state bank, I was not familiar with it. The banker I spoke with on my client's behalf the day before was not listed as an employee at any of their branches adding to my growing sense of unease.

As a courtesy, I called the property owner back to let him know there might be a delay with the offer.

"I'm glad you called,' he said. "I've started getting mail addressed to Vera here at this address."

"What? What are they trying to do?" I wondered aloud.

"I'm very uncomfortable with this," the owner said. "Those two are frauds. I'm pulling my house off the market and calling the police."

The next few minutes were spent scouring the internet for information on Ron and Vera, and what I found infuriated me. It turned out they were wanted in multiple states for fraud, allegedly orchestrating high-end charity events and disappearing with the proceeds. Shockingly, Ron and Vera were not their real names; they operated under multiple aliases.

Adding to the deception, they weren't even married.

It dawned on me that the banker Ron had connected me with was likely just another accomplice in their scheme. Feeling a mixture of frustration and embarrassment, I couldn't help but criticize myself for falling for their deceit. Did Ron and Vera truly believe they could boldly steal a luxury home? Perhaps their plan was to squat in lavish surroundings, explaining why they had mail delivered to the property. Those seemingly innocent photos they were taking during our tour could have been part of a plan to case the property for a potential burglary later on. The audacity of their plan left me both astonished and disheartened.

With a sense of duty, I dialed Ron and Vera's number to inform them that the property was going to be withdrawn from the market and that the owner had requested they cease sending their mail there. Despite knowing more about their deceitful intentions, I chose not to reveal the extent of my knowledge during the call.

Ron quickly changed the subject. "We're going to be hosting a big charity event next month in the area and we'd like you to be the face of it. You would be great. You are heavily involved in your charities. And well-liked too, I imagine. What do you say?"

"I'm very busy. Not sure if I will be available."

"Think about it."

I was not about to take part in one of their charity scams. Feeling manipulated and deceived, I decided to take action. I promptly reached out to my commercial lender who had referred them in the first place, apprising her of the situation.

Understandably, she was shocked by the revelation and advised me to block their number immediately. Realizing the gravity of the situation, I forwarded the driver's license copies they emailed me, along with the fabricated bank letter to a friend who was a police officer. After examining the documents, he confirmed everything was fake and reported it.

As for Ron and Vera, their illicit activities finally caught up with them. The last I heard; they had been extradited to New Mexico to face the consequences of their fraudulent actions.

MENTAL NOTE:
Vet your referrals and trust your instincts.

18

Third Time's a Charm

I f someone is going to buy a property as their primary residence, it is understandable that they would be very particular about every little detail. For a second home, however, a few minor deviations from the ideal would seem acceptable. Over the course of a week, I accompanied my client, Michelle, a doctor, and part-time resident from California, on visits to several homes. Each property closely matched the initial description of her ideal property, but I soon noticed that her criteria for an ideal home were evolving with each viewing. Despite this evolution, some preferences remained consistent. Michelle emphasized that the property must not be subject to an HOA, as she envisioned the possibility of short-term rentals in the future. Additionally, she insisted that the house must have a minimum of three bedrooms and two full baths, criteria that remained unchanged throughout our search.

After an extensive search, we finally found a property that exceeded Michelle's expectations and left her thrilled. Recognizing her excitement, I expedited the paperwork to ensure a swift offer process, allowing her to move forward with her dream home without delay.

"I think you'll be happy with this one," I said.

"We'll see what the home inspector says," she replied.

Having the luxury of no immediate time pressure due to this being a second home did not keep Michelle from facing the dilemma of choosing from a plethora of options. Nevertheless, the home we were placing an offer on appeared promising, adding a sense of urgency to her decision-making process. With the advantage of having the funds available for a cash sale, bypassing the need for lender approval, Michelle was in a favorable position to secure her desired property.

When the inspection report came in, there were a few minor issues found. I forwarded the report to Michelle with a note. *Looks good, just cosmetic items!*

My phone rang.

"What do you mean 'looks good'?" Michelle asked.

"The inspector found a few minor problems. Nothing major. A couple of loose wall sockets, a broken knob on the outside faucet, a wobbly ceiling fan, and the dryer vent needs replacing. Small cosmetic items."

"It sure sounds like a lot of problems to me," Michelle responded.

"It's been my experience that when there are no big issues found during an inspection, the inspector will find small things to write up to show how thorough they are. Really, this house is in great shape considering its age."

"I'd rather keep looking. Let's withdraw the offer."

My heart sank. Here we go again.

Regrettably, sending the buyer inspection notice to the listing agent would be awkward especially since the agent mentioned the seller would repair items. My client, unable to tolerate issues like a loose ceiling fan, has decided to cancel the transaction.

Over the following weeks, during Michelle's visits to town, I continued to show her various properties. After careful consideration, she decided to put an offer on a property not far from her initial choice.

"I like this neighborhood better," Michelle said.

I didn't point out how close we were to the previous house. If Michelle was happy, that's what mattered.

I held my breath as I opened the email with the inspector's report. Again, no major issues, though there were several minor ones. I forwarded the report to Michelle without the *looks good* comment this time. I hoped her love of the house would overcome her concern with the issues found by the inspector.

My phone rang.

"What is it with these sellers that they try to sell a house with so many problems?" she asked. "Front door latch not working properly, water heater pan is missing," she read from the report. "If these obvious problems are present, what hope is there that the seller isn't hiding less obvious problems."

She did have a point, but I knew the inspector would have discovered any major problems with the house. "No house is going to be perfect. We can ask the seller to fix things as a condition of the sale or lower the sale price and you can get them fixed later."

"I'm not in the home repair business," she said.

I could tell from her tone that she was annoyed, so I responded, "Do you want me to contact the seller?"

"No, I want you to withdraw my offer. Let's keep looking."

I found myself at a crossroads: should I part ways with the client and accept the losses, or persist in the hopes that it would eventually lead to a successful purchase? After much deliberation, I opted to stay committed to Michelle. Despite the challenges, we had already made significant progress together, and I had confidence that she would ultimately find a suitable property.

Continuing our search, Michelle and I explored various properties for an additional three weeks, I believe we were up to our forty-third property viewing. *(I have a personal limit of forty-five.)*

"This is nice," Michelle commented as we pulled into the driveway of a white two-story contemporary design with a large covered front porch and an attached two-car garage.

"It's much newer than most of the ones we've looked at," I mentioned.

"Well then, maybe it will have fewer problems."

"Let's hope so."

During our tour of the vacant house, we were immediately struck by its open layout on the main floor, creating a sense of spaciousness despite its small size. Upstairs, the bedrooms continued to impress, with ample space and notable natural light. Stepping outside to the back of the house, we discovered a charming, patterned brick patio and tall privacy fencing, adding to the property's appeal.

"I think I'd like to put an offer on this one," Michelle said.

For the third time in about three months, I filled out the paperwork. I had much of Michelle's personal information memorized already.

As it turned out, the seller had multiple expensive claims on the house and the insurance premiums would be astronomical. There had been a hailstorm and the roof had to be replaced, an electrical fire at the breaker panel caused by lightning, and a municipal sewer backup that flooded the downstairs bathroom.

I was sure Michelle would cancel after learning about this, but her only concern was how high the insurance was going to be. To keep the sale afloat, I offered to contribute part of my commission toward the insurance premium. I guess the third time's a charm, we closed on the property and Michelle was happy!

As a token of appreciation for my clients, I always ensure to present them with thoughtful gifts after the closing as a sincere thank you for their trust and partnership throughout the transaction. Given Michelle's circumstances, with her not planning to occupy the house for the next two months, I decided against arranging a professional house cleaning as part of the post-closing gift. Additionally, I had already contributed part of my commission towards the insurance, ensuring she had one less thing to worry about as she settled into her new home.

Two months later, Michelle called me out of the blue. "The house is filthy. Shouldn't the seller clean it?"

"Well, no," I replied. "You've owned the house for over two months now. Once you own the house, it's your responsibility. I'll send you the name of a reputable cleaning company. That's the best I can do at this point."

After investing significant time and effort, spanning over four months in the difficult process of finding Michelle the perfect home, I made the decision not to undertake any additional work or incur further expenses. Contrary to the sentiment expressed in the Brittany Spears song, "I'm A Slave For You," I want to emphasize that as an agent, I am not here to be enslaved to any demands or expectations. I'm sure she's happy now. Byeee.

MENTAL NOTE:
Persist until you succeed.

19

Surprise, Surprise!

S elling a fixer-upper in a neighborhood where the house is the least attractive property can often be very profitable. By bringing the property up to the standard of nearby homes, you can significantly increase its market value and ensure a good return on your investment.

I showed Justin, a very tall and physically fit ex-military guy with a knack for flipping properties, various project opportunities. Did I mention his impressive biceps, captivating blue eyes, and thick, luscious hair? Wait, this isn't that kind of story.

It was a dreary day to be viewing properties, heavily overcast with a cold January breeze blowing with light rain. There is something about showing properties in bad weather that sets a tone for prospective buyers to say no. Depending on the property, the home's mood can be depressing and dark.

Justin and I visited a few properties within his budget. Regrettably, most were situated in rundown neighborhoods, offering a low purchase-to-resale ratio that made the prospect of renovation seem unprofitable. None of the houses appeared suitable for his needs.

In the late afternoon, we arrived at our final destination: a neglected and overgrown house on Crescent Drive. Undoubtedly, this property stood out as the one diminishing property values in the neighborhood due to its sorry state. The surrounding houses were modest yet well-maintained, placed on small rectangular lots. The neighborhood was located in an older part of the city, but these homes had a mid-twentieth-century charm, complemented by lush, mature vegetation.

"*Nice* neighborhood," Justin remarked. "Nothing pretentious. Very livable."

I thought he sounded like a listing brochure, so I added, "Walking distance to shopping, restaurants, an elementary school, and bus stop."

We stepped out of the vehicle. From the street, we could see windows covered on the inside with aluminum foil.

"What's with the tinfoil shades?" Justin joked, "Is the government reading our brain waves?"

"I don't remember the foil being there when I showed this a couple of months ago to another investor. It's been on the market for quite a while."

"Squatters?" Justin asked.

"It wouldn't surprise me," I responded.

"Don't worry. I always carry Ol' Trusty." He patted the gun in its holster on his hip.

"I hope we won't be needing that," I said, though I wasn't unhappy Justin carried.

I opened the mechanical lockbox for the key and as I approached the door to insert it, the door creaked open slightly. "Unlocked," I remarked. It wasn't uncommon for agents to forget to secure properties, but my instincts tingled with caution. A toxic odor seeped through the crack of the slightly ajar door, a mix of cat urine and cigarette stench. I retrieved two masks from my blazer pocket, though Justin opted not to use one.

I was apprehensive, so I asked Justin to go in first.

"Sure," he said, "we're not in Kandahar."

As I trailed closely behind him, it felt as though we were navigating through a haunted house or a scary corn maze at the county fair, half-expecting someone to leap out from around the corner and unleash a piercing scream. The interior was cloaked in darkness, with windows obscured by foil and broken light bulbs hanging from their fixtures. We hurried through the rooms as fast as possible while Justin thought out loud about the potential of the property. Dirty dishes and food scraps littered the kitchen counters though the place was vacant. In various rooms, old-fashioned furniture lay scattered about, some of it toppled over or positioned randomly. The home's set up reminded me of the scene in Breaking Bad with the ATM. Once I thought of this episode a rush came over me, like something bad was about to happen.

In the dimly lit living room, a large rolled-up area rug lay in one corner, accompanied by a heap of small boxes. The space reeked of hasty departure, reminiscent of a chilling scene from a horror film. Suddenly, a deep grunt sprang from the concealed depths of the rug, causing me to startle violently. Without hesitation, Justin's hand instinctively gravitated towards his holster, ready to confront whatever lurked in the shadows. "I have a gun," he shouted. "Whoever you are, you are trespassing."

The squatter, a short man with a long graying beard and crazed bulging eyes, rose on all fours then lunged toward us with a knife in his hand. The man screamed something at us, it was all a blur and happening so fast. I just recall hearing a loud sound, like a possum squealing.

With the assailant closing in on us, Justin issued another

stern warning before quickly drawing his gun and firing a shot into the man's chest. I stood frozen in shock, watching as the knife slipped from the man's grasp, clanking to the floor. Gripping his chest in agony, the man staggered forward, collapsing with a heavy thud just steps away from where we stood. Blood softly splattered across my left cheek, and in that moment, time seemed to halt, everything unfolding in slow motion as a deafening ring echoed in my ears. I turned to Justin, my voice trembling as I posed the question, "Is he... dead?" Justin nodded in affirmation.

Still twirling from shock, I bolted outside, unable to bear the nasty odor any longer, desperately needing a moment to collect my thoughts and process the disturbing events that had just transpired. Taking a couple of deep breaths to calm down, my hands trembling, I dialed 911.

Justin came out and stood near me shaking his head.

"100% dead?" I asked.

"No pulse," he answered. His gun was back in its holster.

"I guess I'll call the listing Agent now. This will be fun," I said in disbelief.

As we waited in the front yard by the porch, a whirlwind of scenarios raced through my mind. What if Justin hadn't been there? I might have faced a fatal stabbing. Lost in my thoughts, I paced around, attempting to dial the listing agent's number, oblivious to the rain pelting my head. Despite being in a state of fight or flight, I found an unexpected calmness, likely due to the shock coursing through me. After several attempts, I managed to dial the correct number, only to be met with a voicemail. Leaving a mangled message on the agent's voicemail,

I anxiously awaited a prompt reply, uncertain of what exactly I had managed to convey in my hurried communication.

When the two police officers arrived, they secured the scene and took our statements separately. They had us wait on the front porch, while they did their write ups.

They returned to the porch.

"The coroner is on her way. That individual is known to us. We've had problems with him before. In fact, we've been looking for him on theft and drug charges."

I was ready for this to be over. "Do you need anything else from us?" I asked the officer.

"I think we're good. Get on with your day."

"Thank you."

We entrusted the officers with the responsibility of awaiting the coroner's arrival. They assured us that they would secure the house once their duties were fulfilled, and they had already informed the seller who was on the way. Personally, I had no inclination to lay eyes on the deceased. Frankly, the prospect of presenting this property again to Justin, should he express interest in purchasing it, filled me with dread. It was unfathomable that we had just been involved in a shooting incident, yet the authorities permitted us to continue with our day as if nothing had happened.

Once in the car, Justin looked at me. "You alright?"

"Yes," I assured him. I had to maintain my composure; I couldn't afford to appear frightened in front of such an attractive man. "I just need a little time to process this. It's not every day something like this happens."

"I should hope not," he said, laughing. "And it's not every

day you sell a house that someone was killed in right before your own eyes. I want to put an offer in for this place."

"Really?"

"Really." He smiled.

I love my clients.

Mental Note: Keep your head on a swivel.

20

Are You Sure About That?

A recent addition to my client base, Erick, owned a modern sixteen-unit townhome complex situated in the bustling entertainment district. Although property management wasn't my primary focus, I occasionally took on leasing. The current property manager for his building was inundated with responsibilities, prompting Erick, who resided out of state, to request my assistance in renting two of the larger units. Having previously collaborated with Erick on various ventures, he entrusted me with this task.

I contacted the property manager, Carmella, to acquire descriptions of the two units: a two-bedroom and a three-bedroom. Although she couldn't provide images of the specific units, Carmella assured me that all units of the same size shared identical layouts.

The three-bedroom townhome was currently occupied, and the tenant's lease was nearing its expiration. Unfortunately, the tenant consistently refused us entry, making it impossible to physically inspect the property. As a result, I only had photos available for reference.

I walked the vacant two-bedroom unit and had a professional photographer snap new photos. The following day, I hosted an open house and experienced a significant amount of foot traffic. Shortly after posting the units online, I received an inquiry for the three-bedroom unit. Three college students, two enrolled in law school and one in medical school, expressed interest in leasing the unit while they attended the nearby university.

"I'm so glad we finally found a place where we could each have our own room," Will told me. "It's been crazy trying to study packed together."

"I completely understand," I replied. As we spoke, I thought he sounded like a responsible young man. His two roommates, listening in on the speakerphone, said hello, but otherwise, let Will do the talking. I let Carmella know I'd found potential tenants and to send them the rental application. Will's father's name was used on the lease since he was the paying party and co-signer. Whatever arrangement he had with the other two was not my concern. It was in Carmella's hands now.

As their move-in day approached, I did a walk-through to confirm it was clean and no items were left behind by the previous tenant, only to find the property manager had made an error. The apartment the boys' lease had been signed for was not a three-bedroom unit as I was told. It was a two bedroom.

I alerted Carmella and Erick. Unfortunately, there were no three bedrooms available for the next two months.

I had to break the news to Will and his friends.

"I feel terrible, but the owner has an offer. He is willing to let you have the two-bedroom for two months rent-free until a three-bedroom becomes available, and you can move into that." I waited while he discussed this with the other two. I could hear considerable pushback until he muted the phone. When Will unmuted, he said, "OK, we'll take it."

Feeling relieved, I promptly informed Erick and the property manager, Carmella, about the decision. Carmella proceeded to update the lease accordingly, and they moved forward with finalizing the two-bedroom unit.

Fast forward about three weeks. I received a call from the Property manager. "Yvonne, those boys are bothering the other tenants. I've gotten several complaints."

"Complaints about what?" I asked. She seemed like she needed to vent, and I ended up being the chosen one.

"You name it. There are wild late-night parties, loud music, drunken individuals urinating over the balcony railing, and trash left in the hallways. Their guests haphazardly park, obstructing other residents. Some tenants have had to resort to towing cars just to leave for work. Yelling matches erupt late at night, and the pervasive smell of weed lingers everywhere. I fear it could escalate into something even more serious!"

"Are you sure it's the students in 1006?" I asked. I struggled to believe that the nice medical and law students, or their friends, would behave in such a manner.

"Positive," Carmella replied. "I have other tenants who want to know if we are kicking those guys out because if not, they want out of their leases. That's how bad it is. We've even called the cops several times, but it doesn't help."

I think Carmella wanted me to handle the situation, although it was clearly within her responsibilities as the property manager. The owner and Carmella were in charge of screening applicants, while I facilitated finding prospects. Unfortunately, it seems I unknowingly handed over a nightmare. It was the property management company's duty to conduct background and financial checks, but it appears they may have been negligent due to the urgency to fill vacancies. I suspect the owner, who had only recently acquired the complex, reduced the number of property managers, leaving those remaining overburdened and compelled to take shortcuts wherever possible.

"Doesn't their lease say something about maintaining the property and respecting the rights of other tenants?" I asked.

"Well, it's complicated. Right now, the father of one of the students is suing the owner and the management company."

"For what?"

"Misrepresenting the rental property and having a lease signed for an unavailable property."

"But they got two months free rent," I argued. "And they agreed to it in writing."

"Apparently, they are claiming their grades have suffered because they do not each have a private room in which to study."

"Really? I wonder if that father knows about the wild parties," I said. "This sounds like a mess, Carmella. I will give the boys a call, but there isn't much I can do. I hope Erick can get them out. Good luck." I hung up and talked myself into not getting too involved. My calls were unanswered by the boys.

I heard from Carmella a couple of months later when she called to ask if I could help find tenants for a couple of units in a different part of the complex. I was a little surprised, being that I felt somewhat responsible for the previous tenant issues.

"So, whatever happened with the wild students?" I asked.

"Gone. Erick was able to prove they violated their lease agreement and kicked them out."

"And what about the lawsuit?"

"Once the father, the one that was a lawyer, saw some of the videos turned over by other tenants showing the boys during their parties, he dropped it."

"Great. What a headache that whole mess was for you."

"Well, I was in a hurry to get that unit rented, so I kind of just sent the lease. I learned my lesson. Just because people seem nice, don't skimp on the background checks."

"I think we all learned something with this one. I will always walk units before posting them anywhere. Triple check everything!"

MENTAL NOTE:
If you want something done right, do it yourself.

21

The HOA

My phone rang. I checked the caller ID, Peter Wilson. I sold a swanky resort condo on a beautiful golf course to him a couple of years ago. I wondered what he could want.

"Peter, so nice to hear from you. In the market for a new house?" I asked, half joking.

"Actually, I might be. The HOA here is going crazy."

"Uh, oh. What's going on there?"

"Have you ever heard of a community within an HOA where the monthly fee is randomly fluctuating? A $50 to $200 a month difference!"

"Do they say why it's going up?" I asked.

"Not just up. Up. Down, Every month it's a surprise. When I moved in, the fee was $300 a month. It stayed that way for a long time. Then it went up to $485, then $550, then down to $510, then--"

"That is really strange," I said. "What did the HOA say?"

"I've left messages. No one gets back. My neighbors don't seem that concerned.

I believe they are more preoccupied with golf or have greater financial means than I do. They don't appear to be bothered by the mismanagement of the property, the poor condition of the parking lot, or the frequent presence of unusual guests at the hotel. But let me refocus. My primary concern is the exorbitant HOA fee."

"Let me look into it."

I made several attempts to contact the HOA representative. I thought being a real estate broker might have more success than a complaining condo owner. Yeah right.

Finally, the representative returned my call and explained that the fees change based on water usage.

"For each owner's usage or community usage?" I asked.

"Hold on," he said and put me on hold. I had the feeling he was conferring with someone higher up. The condo was one of dozens in a golfing community situated on 15 acres behind a hotel which waters their greens frequently. But that still doesn't make sense. These owners are not watering crops or filling an Olympic sized pool every other day!

When he returned, he asked, "Where were we?" Was he hoping I had forgotten my question?

"I asked if the water fee was charged based on an individual's use or averaged out across the community."

There was a pause. "That, I don't know. Fees are charged based on water usage," he repeated.

"But they didn't used to," I said. "Why now?"

"I've told you what I know," he replied. "Have a good day."

Did he just hang up on me? WTH!

When I relayed the news to Peter, he decided to have me list his condo. Luckily the market at the time was moving and I was able to sell it to an investor who wanted it for a vacation rental. Even though the HOA was lame, there were no rental restrictions – perfect for short-term leasing.

MENTAL NOTE:
Buyer beware.

22

Material Facts

I represented the Reynolds family as their buyer's agent—a delightful family comprising a mother, father, and two young boys. Their priority was finding a home with a spacious yard for the kids to enjoy. We spent a couple of weeks exploring different properties to find the perfect fit.

"They all have great yards, but the houses aren't a good layout for us," Devin Reynolds said. "We need something more open so Sarah can keep an eye on the boys while she works."

"Working from home is great, but not if I have to get up every five minutes to check on them," Sarah explained.

I scanned the listings on my phone. "Maybe this next one will fit the bill. It's in a newer development built on former farmland about ten years ago. It's been on the market for a while and that works in our favor when making an offer."

We followed the GPS directions and soon arrived at a well-kept stucco house with a large, covered porch and attached two-car garage. It was similar to the other houses we passed in the development.

"I'm liking the one story, Yvonne," Sarah said. "No worries about the kids falling down the stairs."

As we toured, both Devin and Sarah commented on the open layout. There was a workspace between the kitchen and living room with a half-wall separating it. The dining room was off the kitchen to the right with an eat-at counter between them.

"Perfect," said Sarah, standing at the work desk. "I can see everything from here."

I saw Devin looking down at the floor in the kitchen. I followed his gaze and saw the long crack in the tiles running along the wall.

"That doesn't look good," he said.

"That happens sometimes as new construction settles," I assured him. "Let me look into it." I snapped a photo.

We walked through the bedrooms finding more cracks, this time in the walls and ceilings. More photos. I could sense their unease. I took them out the patio doors and we walked around in the roomy backyard. At the back edge of the property, I looked toward the house. There was something about the roofline that looked off like the house wasn't quite level. These subdivisions built on farmland could be prone to stability issues. I tried to convince myself I was imagining it but added it to my list of things to check on. My intuition was telling me something was seriously wrong with the property.

"Are those broken tiles on the roof?" asked Devin, pointing to the area above the garage.

"They sure are," I answered, walking closer and pulling out my phone to take photos.

After their initial positive feelings about the property, I sensed a hesitation.

"I want more information. Get what the deal is on those cracks," Devin said.

"I'm with you on that. I will get back to you ASAP," I replied.

Once back at the office, I researched the builder and looked at the property photos/details more closely. Turned out that the listing agent had invested in this house with the owner hoping to make a good flip. I recalled past dealings with that agent.

Always trying to give a small payment *(Flat rate less than 1%)* to the buyer's agent so he can keep more for himself. Always looking to cut corners. He reminded me of the saying, *I wouldn't buy a used car from that man.* Now, the situation isn't so dire since the commission structure is set to change because of the National Association's involvement. Sellers won't be responsible for paying a commission to the buyer's agent anymore. This development made national headlines; even the President of the United States discussed it on television.

Armed with this knowledge, I called the listing agent. He assured me the house was solid and emailed me a copy of the last inspection done for a buyer who recently canceled. As it turned out, the cracks in the foundation were only one part of the problem. There was also an issue with the trusses.

I called the agent back. "I see the previous buyer backed out after this inspection. What's with the trusses?"

"Oh that," he said, chuckling. "The roof is new and that is just from the weight of the guys working on it."

I didn't believe that explanation for a moment. He was clearly being deceptive, attempting to unload the property while conveniently omitting crucial details—something that could jeopardize his license. He underestimated me, assuming I'd buy into his ignorance, but I saw through his charade. I've encountered his type before—they'll say whatever suits the buyer's desires to seal the deal.

My clients decided they wanted to put in an offer notwithstanding their initial hesitation and before hearing about the inspection report. The layout was exactly what they were looking for, and they were afraid they might lose out if they didn't act quickly. Devin was confident they could handle any repairs. I thought otherwise.

"I don't recommend buying this house." I shared the inspection that had been completed for the previous buyer, the one who subsequently backed out. "I will feel responsible If that roof falls on you, or something happens to your family. But more than that, if you did buy it, I wouldn't be able to sleep worrying about any *what ifs*. And if something did happen, I couldn't live with myself."

Devin and Sarah decided to keep looking.

"I'm sure we'll find something that suits your needs," I assured them.

"And one that won't fall on our heads," added Sarah.

MENTAL NOTE:
A solid foundation lays the groundwork
for everything.

23

Door Number Three

S howing occupied homes can cause some anxiety. I'm not fond of encountering closed doors leading to bedrooms or bathrooms because the mystery behind them can be unsettling.

On the day I scheduled several showings for my clients Janice and Steve, the weather, predicted to be cloudy, turned into a series of strong thunderstorms. Janice and Steve were not deterred.

The homes they had chosen to view were all in the three to five-million range, and all had their minimum requirement of six bedrooms and at least a four-car garage. They were open to view homes with a range of layouts, but the primary closet size was non-negotiable. The bigger the better.

"We'll know it when we see it," said Janice. "It will speak to us."

"And if not, we'll consider the best option," added Steve, adding a note of pragmatism.

We had a productive morning. They had good things to say about each of the properties.

After lunch at a trendy restaurant which they insisted on paying for, we headed for house number five on our list.

Luckily, the storms let up before we arrived. The listing agent was not going to meet us for this showing but assured me the house would be vacant. The seller was in the process of moving out, and his visiting in-laws will be out for the day.

We approached the front door. No lockbox. I grabbed the

door handle. It was locked, of course. I checked my phone for the showing instructions to confirm the lockbox location. It said the front door. This was awkward. Nothing like feeling foolish in front of clients. We looked around like an Easter egg hunt and located the lockbox in a large planter just lying there attached to nothing.

The home was magnificent. The two-story front foyer had staircases cascading down on either side of a balcony and around an oversized crystal chandelier that was truly breathtaking. The marble floors throughout and the incredible woodwork gave it both a modern feel and very classic.

The first floor was empty except for a few stacks of boxes and a gigantic arched sectional in the middle of the living room. Most of the owner's furniture had been removed. Normally a property of this magnitude would be staged, but if the market is hot, it may sell before that is necessary. This property had only been on the market for a few days. It was easy to imagine the rooms with furniture. The formal dining room, eat-in kitchen, family room, living room, and office were all considerable and airy.

The second floor was my nightmare scenario. Every door was closed. I could feel my heart beating. I convinced myself that my anxiety was just from watching too many murder mysteries and hoarder flip shows combined with my very wild imagination.

Janice, Steve, and I checked the first two bedrooms and shared bathroom. Like downstairs, they were empty except for already packed boxes.

As we got to the door of bedroom number three down the

hall across from the open-concept foyer, we heard weird sounds like a dying cat or animal in pain.

"What in the world was that?" whispered Janice.

I texted the listing agent. Are you sure no one is here?

I got an almost instant reply. The in-laws' golf game was canceled due to weather, and they may not have gotten the memo about the showing...

My intuition told me to leave, but we really wanted to see the primary bedroom. We had to see the closet for Janice's sake. It was clear someone was inside the room, so I announced myself.

"Is anyone there? This is Yvonne, I'm here with my clients to show the house."

No response.

As I was reading a second text from the agent, the doorknob turned from inside. The door swung open and a sweaty little naked man wearing nipple clamps among other things surprised us. I couldn't look away; it was like seeing a car accident and we could not unsee what was coming toward us. Over his shoulder, a woman was sitting up on a mattress, covering herself with a sheet. It was obvious the in-laws had been fooling around. I'm just thankful we didn't see them in full action.

"I'm so sorry! We were told the house would be vacant," I said, looking away. My clients were already moving toward the stairs at a fast pace.

The man started laughing and called out after us, "We lost track of time. But hopefully you like the house. Make an offer, my son needs to sell!"

We left without seeing the entire home. My clients had seen

enough.

I followed up with the agent, and the seller was mortified by his in-laws' activities. No one was hurt during this showing, but my clients and I are scarred for life. They ended up purchasing a different home, but we will always have the fun memory of door number three.

MENTAL NOTE:
Always listen to your intuition.

24

What's That Smell?

Claudia, so nice to hear from you," I said. Claudia couldn't see my smile over the phone, but I bet she could sense it. Claudia and I go back many years. She is the kindest lady and over those years purchased multiple properties as rental investments. She is very savvy at it. "What can I do for you?" I asked.

"You know that single-family home on Oakview I bought through you. I think it was my second purchase."

"The one with the picket fence?" I responded, trying to refresh my memory.

"That's the one, only that old fence is long gone. I'm interested in selling it now. Properties in that vicinity have been fetching considerably higher prices recently."

"There is a bit of urban revitalization in that neighborhood. I think it's a smart move to sell now."

"I want to get in on that bubble," Claudia continued. "It's such a great location with downtown in walking distance."

"A great selling point. Close to entertainment and dining. Home values are skyrocketing. I agree, now is a good time to sell."

"Thank you, Yvonne. The trouble is, I can't make it back there to see what it needs before I put it on the market. Is that something you could do for me? I wouldn't ask normally, but the tenants are a nice family. Mom, Dad, and a little girl. They've been tenants for a couple of years and have been no trouble, although the rent has been late a couple of times recently.

They're on a month-to-month lease now and I've already given them a sixty-day notice to vacate."

"For you, Claudia, of course."

I called the number Claudia gave me and spoke with Robert, her tenant. We arranged a time for me to inspect the property. He sounded slightly nervous, but I didn't pay attention to it at the time. Claudia had vouched for the family, so I went alone this time, which isn't my usual practice.

I arrived at the house. It seemed smaller than I remember, but maybe the picket fence had made it seem bigger. It was a single-story two-bedroom home. A brief glance as I arrived made it clear that the exterior white paint needed refreshing. The lawn had patches of dry grass and bare spots. On the lawn, amidst various toys, there was a small bike equipped with training wheels and a child's plastic shopping cart filled with plastic groceries. I took note of the landscaping that needed attention.

Robert was waiting outside to meet me. I parked and walked up to greet him. He was barefoot, wearing a faded AC/DC t-shirt and stained baggy dark pants.

"Hi, I'm Yvonne," I said. "I won't take much of your time."

"Okay. It's just me here right now. Kate and the little one are at the store."

He led me inside. We walked from room to room. I smelled a peculiar odor but could not place it. The rooms were messy, like they hadn't bothered to tidy up even knowing I was coming. I would have thought he lived there alone, but women's and children's things were all over the place. There were numerous Glade plugins throughout, but the odor wasn't from them. It was stronger and unpleasant. I could feel my eyes stinging.

The dim lighting in the rooms didn't obscure the fact that the floors would require a thorough cleaning, and in certain areas, replacement might be necessary, particularly the kitchen tiles.

As we entered the primary bedroom, Robert seemed on edge. The room wasn't any messier than the others and I wasn't sure why he seemed so tense. I tried not to show that he was making me nervous, but my senses were on high alert.

I did notice the odor was getting stronger as we approached the primary bathroom. The door was closed, I reached for the handle and Robert lunged to block me from grabbing the knob. I was alarmed and immediately regretted my decision to come alone!

"Sorry. Sorry. I'm sorry," he repeated. "It's a real mess in there. You can't see it today."

As he spoke, I couldn't escape the strong odor. It smelled of chemicals and cat urine. It was stinging my nostrils, and I could feel a headache coming on. I'm thinking to myself, *Where I have, smelled this before?* Then it dawned on me. It smelled like a house I showed clients a couple of years earlier. Which turned out to be a meth house. *Is this guy cooking meth? I was shaken,* but I just smiled and said, "I understand. Is all the plumbing working? No leaks or anything broken?"

"No. It's all good."

"Okay. Well, I think that's all I need for today." I walked back through the house with Robert following. At the door, I thanked him and made a beeline to my car. That was the fastest house tour of my career. I couldn't imagine a family living with that odor, especially a child.

As soon as Robert went inside his house, I removed my shoes and put them in a plastic bag in the trunk. I slipped on my spare flipflops. My trunk of supplies came in handy once again.

I used a dry-cleaning bag to cover the driver's seat and kept the windows open on the way home. Even then I could smell the overpowering odor on my clothes.

By the time I got home, my eyes were red and puffy, my nose was running and I was coughing non-stop. I parked in my garage, stripped off my clothes, and threw them in the trash. I used sanitizer to wipe down anywhere I had touched the car. After a few minutes, my coughing had calmed.

After showering, I called my client and recounted my visit to the house.

"Oh, my. I was not expecting that," Claudia gasped.

"I'm pretty sure Robert has a meth lab in the main bathroom. I recommend calling the police and get him out of there."

"I'll call my brother to check it out. He's a retired police sergeant for the city."

"I remember meeting him when you still lived in the area."

A couple of days later, I got a call from Claudia. "You were correct. Robert had a meth lab in my house. My brother said the giveaway before he even entered was the patches of dead grass on the lawn. It's where they dump the used chemicals. I can't believe it. I suppose you never really know with some people. Well, Robert's been arrested and is sitting in jail right now."

"I feel bad for his family. I hope his wife and daughter get the assistance they need."

"I spoke with Kate this morning. She and Missy will be

staying with relatives. Staying in that house, breathing that air, is too dangerous."

"Thank goodness they have somewhere to go." I was relieved.

"On the bright side, renovations can start right away."

Claudia had the house professionally remediated and renovated over the next few months, and despite its past, we did find a buyer who purchased it as a rental property. Hopefully, he will have better tenants.

MENTAL NOTE:
Be cautious of an overabundance of Glade plugins.

25

Peace Love Joy

Phillip reached out, expressing interest in purchasing investment properties. Just like everyone else I know.

"Fixer-uppers that will bring in good rents," he said. "I'm not afraid of major renovation work."

It just so happened that my agent friend mentioned to me that he had a client considering selling his three adjacent houses on the same street, all owned by the same family.

"You might be interested in these. They are not on the market yet," I said. I proceeded to describe the listings.

Phillip provided me with his information and proof of funds, he planned to pay cash. I set up a tentative date to view the properties with my agent friend, *let's call him Bob.*

We were the first ones to see the homes, all were tenant occupied and not easy to schedule. We stood outside the houses on the sidewalk across the busy main street.

The houses were in a prime location, with proximity to shopping, restaurants, and offices. All three properties were single-story homes situated on medium-sized lots, suggesting they might have been constructed by the same builder several decades ago. However, the properties were currently in a state of disrepair.

All had cracked driveways, overgrown shrubs, worn roofs, and missing pieces of siding. The middle house even had a seven-foot-tall gold spray painted statue of a seated Buddha in the middle of the front yard. In the window, a small sign read *Peace Love Joy.*

"No HOA here," Phillip said, pointing to the statue.

"That's for sure," I replied.

We toured each of the houses with Bob leading the way. The tenants in the first house were polite and let us walk through without interruption.

House number two was a different story. The tenant, Miss Aurora, did not want to let us in until we proved who we were and that we weren't the police.

Once inside the cluttered home, it was obvious she had set up an illegal retail store in her front room and kitchen area. She had shelves of crystals, candles, prayer flags, various brass, and wooden incense burners, one which was filling the air with pungent sage fragrance. There were dreamcatchers, beaded necklaces, and bracelets, as well as trinkets of all kinds on the counters. A handwritten poster on the wall listed prices for massages, yoga classes, and daycare. Miss Aurora herself was dressed in flowing tie dye jumpsuit and dangling gold earrings.

Clearly distressed, she trailed us, repeatedly asking, "So, who's gonna buy this house and kick me out on the street?"

Bob politely reminded her that the current owner had the right to inspect the home's condition and requested privacy for our viewing. Her demeanor exuded intense negativity. I thought to myself, she has a sign on the front of her house that reads "Peace Love Joy," As Maury Povich would say, "The lie detector determined that was a lie!"

The layout of the house mirrored the first, and it appeared to be in a similar state of disrepair. However, it was challenging to assess the condition of the walls due to the large, tie-dyed sheets and tapestries covering them. One of the bedrooms was cluttered with toys, and we noticed two preschool children napping on small beds, so we avoided disturbing them.

House number three was in a much more deteriorated state than the other two. The tenant was a middle-aged man who only used one of the bedrooms, the other areas were for storage.

"The landlord gave me a break on the rent if he could use two of the rooms for storage," he said. The backyard was a mess, with holes dug up everywhere—courtesy of the adorable puppy he had recently acquired.

As we exited the house, away from Bob's hearing range, my new client expressed eagerness and said, "Let's put in an offer. These have potential."

As soon as Phillip closed, we gave the tenants a sixty-day notice to vacate. When we arrived at the properties to do a more thorough inspection, Miss Aurora accused us of forcing her and her children onto the streets. Despite her accusations, she did move out on schedule. However, reflecting on this situation, I can't help but feel concerned about potential karmic consequences.

As soon as the homes were empty, we started the renovations. I helped Phillip with renovation designs. Construction was slowed by the difficulty of finding contractors and supply chain issues due to the pandemic.

During this period, the market experienced a shift due to high interest rates, causing the homes to linger on the market. As they remained vacant, homeless individuals began to congregate around the properties, seeking shelter.

My client hired a security team to walk the areas on a nightly basis. They caught many characters and turned them over to the police. Over twenty-five incidents in four months. From young kids caught with drugs, homeless trying to break in, to thieves trying to steal copper pipes. What a mess!

One evening, while the security team was present, a man was standing on the driveway of house number one. He showed the security guys a cashier's check for $6000, explaining, "Yvonne, the agent on the sign, will give me keys today. I signed a lease and I have her money."

One of the guys called me immediately and I assured him that was not the case.

As they were waiting there together, the "imposter Yvonne" drove by slowly. The man shouted, "That's her! That's the car."

She sped off.

It transpired that the house had been listed on Craigslist by this woman. Luckily the man hadn't given her his deposit, and the lease he signed was totally invalid.

He asked if he could rent it from us, but he thought the rent was the $1000 a month which is what the imposter woman told him. It was actually listed for $5000 a month, way over his budget.

Since the rental aspect wasn't proving successful, Phillip made the decision to list them for sale. However, the mortgage rates kept climbing, homeless individuals continued to trespass, and no buyers seemed to be on the horizon. Despite pricing the properties competitively, affordability had changed. As I reflect on these challenges, I can only hope that by the time this book goes to print, the homes will have been sold. Wish us luck!

MENTAL NOTE:
Timing is everything!

EPILOGUE

As we wrap up this rollercoaster ride through the quirky and interesting world of real estate, I want to leave you with more than just a few laughs and raised eyebrows. In this epilogue, consider it my final sales pitch – not for a property, but for a perspective.

Beyond the humor, weirdness, and lightheartedness, lies a deep experience-based understanding of this industry's peaks, valleys, and all the nuances in between. Whether you're an aspiring agent, a potential buyer, or simply in search of a chuckle, remember this: in the dynamic world of real estate, every transaction presents its own set of challenges and positive outcomes. Success in real estate isn't solely determined by closing deals; it's about adeptly maneuvering through the unpredictable terrain, prioritizing client satisfaction, and finding amusement in the unexpected twists and turns along the way.

Thank you for joining me on this comical journey I call my career.

About the Author

Yvonne M., an experienced real estate broker adept at handling the unforeseeable outcomes of transactions, steps into the literary spotlight with a dark comedic flair. Drawing from years of firsthand experiences in the competitive and occasionally quirky real estate industry, Yvonne injects a distinctive approach into the high-stakes game of buying and selling properties.

Originally from Ontario, Canada, Yvonne grew up as the only child in a family with Czech roots. Her inspiration stems from her immigrant parents and a strong commitment to

community service. Recognized for her dedication to local charities and volunteering, Yvonne believes in going above and beyond in every aspect of life. This commitment was further reinforced by a couple of near-death experiences she faced before obtaining her real estate license. Recognizing the uncertainty of tomorrow, Yvonne lives by the mantra of giving her best in all endeavors.

Facing a pivotal moment after a near-fatal car accident, Yvonne found herself pondering the path ahead during her year-long recovery. Despite the limitations imposed by her injuries, she humorously reflects on the decision-making process: "What else do you do with your life when you don't know what else to do? Get your Real Estate license!" This unexpected situation led her to a new chapter, blending her resilience, humor, and passion for real estate into a compelling journey.

When she isn't orchestrating deals or crafting witty narratives, you'll catch Yvonne on the golf course, DJ-ing at local venues, volunteering or enjoying leisurely strolls with her furry companion. With her literary debut, Yvonne extends a heartfelt invitation for readers to laugh, cringe, and empathize with the ups and downs of the real estate rollercoaster.